90 Powis Crescent.

THE TRUMPET SOUNDS FOR BRITAIN

The
Trumpet Sounds
for Britain

Volume 1
Revival or Perish

David E. Gardner

CHRISTIAN FOUNDATION PUBLICATIONS
45 Appleton Road, Hale, Altrincham, Cheshire

Unless otherwise stated, biblical quotations are from
the Authorised (King James) Version

Publishing Consultants and Phototypesetting
Nuprint Services Limited, Harpenden, Hertfordshire

Printed in Great Britain for
CHRISTIAN FOUNDATION PUBLICATIONS
45 Appleton Road, Hale, Altrincham, Cheshire by
Purnell & Sons (Book Production) Ltd., Paulton, Somerset

Contents

Foreword

by Sir Cyril Black, JP, DL, FRICS, FAI
(formerly MP for Wimbledon)

I am privileged to have been invited by my dear friend the
Rev. David Gardner to contribute a foreword to Volume
1 of his latest book – *The Trumpet Sounds for Britain*,
which is intended to be followed in due course by two
further volumes.

This is, and is intended to be, a deeply disturbing book,
and should most certainly be read by the increasing
number of our fellow citizens who are deeply concerned
at the obvious moral and spiritual decline of our nation,
and its lessening influence in the world. Many such people
cannot understand why our country, with its great history,
and its triumph in 1945 (when in 1940 we had stood alone
faced with what seemed to be certain defeat) has since
suffered such unmitigated disasters.

The author makes clear that our decline has inexorably
taken place over a very much longer period, and, for
reasons which he clearly and carefully analyses, has
brought us to the verge of disaster.

Some facile optimists still believe 'all's well with the
world'. Such people have always existed since the days of
Noah, but this attitude of mind and heart will not save
them from impending disaster, any more than it saved
mankind at the time of the flood.

This book is a careful analysis of the rises and falls in
our nation's history since early times over long centuries,
and explains the reasons why in some periods we have
triumphed, and in others been cast down.

Not all readers, Christians and others, will totally agree
in every particular with the author's reading of history, or
with every detail of his stirring call. Our long island story
contains episodes on which history seems clouded and
doubtful, and of which the records are not clear. But this
in no way invalidates the author's main conclusions which,

I am convinced, are soundly based.

On the main thesis I have no doubt.

Can we not all agree that God has shown great forebearance to our nation, and showered blessings upon us; that he has made it plain that he has a special purpose and destiny ordained for us; that at times when we have obeyed him and walked in the paths of righteousness he has blessed us; that when we have rebelled he has chastised us; that our profound influence in some periods of history has not been due to our wealth or power, but our faithfulness to God; that in this period of decline in which we live today our condition is grave, and due to our neglect of the laws of a just and righteous God, and our rejection of his Son, our Lord and Saviour Jesus Christ?

The day is dark, and the hour is late, but even at the eleventh hour it is still gloriously possible for us to turn defeat into victory.

God's faithful remnant has in days past wonderfully triumphed when all seemed lost.

The new birth, made possible by Christ's death on the cross, is offered to all 'without money and without price'. This is the 'one thing' that most of our people lack.

Through this book the trumpet has sounded its clarion call. Let us take courage and go forward in the name of the Lord, trusting in his strength.

This is the hour when in a special way the witness of every individual Christian counts. Readers of this book, by the very act of reading, will assume a new responsibility, for their duty will have been made clear and plain.

The crisis is desperate and the days are dark, but sometimes the darkest hour is just before the dawn.

My prayer for many years past, and today, is that I may be spared to behold the coming of revival to our beloved land.

May all readers work and pray for the early coming of that great day 'when the kingdoms of this world will become the kingdom of our Lord and of his Christ.'

Introduction

There is abundant evidence to show that the hand of God has been on the history of this country from its very earliest beginnings, and at work on its behalf in at least five ways by

1) constituting us an island (or group of islands);
2) giving us Christian foundations;
3) preserving those Christian foundations whenever they have been in danger of being lost or destroyed;
4) ensuring that our laws are based on the Bible; and
5) bringing about mighty acts of deliverance.

These facts are quite irrefutable, and are explored in the first seven chapters of the book.

The author then moves to the present day. Since issuing his *A Warning to the Nation* in 1969, he has watched with concern and alarm Britain's spiritual and moral situation deteriorate unarrested. He warned then of the very real danger of a judgment of God falling upon Britain in terms of a 'takeover' by the enemy from without. He now sees this as imminent, and hence the urgent need to 'sound the trumpet' for Britain.

The author makes an assessment of Britain's present crisis from a study of similar situations which occur in the Bible. He finds that Britain's real trouble, as a nation which has been singularly blessed by God in past days, is not only that she has departed from God and is, in fact, now going directly against him and so is already incurring his judgments. He sees very clearly that Britain has also gone exactly the same way that the Old Testament nation of Israel went – if not further – and is therefore likely to suffer the same consequences which, in Israel's case, was a judgment of God at the hands of an invading enemy army. With the alarming increase in the Soviet military build-up forming the ingredients of that kind of judgment, the author considers that this is a very real possibility for Britain in the next few years, and sees the urgent need, like Ezekiel, 'to sound the trumpet and warn the people' (Ezekiel 33:1-7). With the enemy almost at the gates, the author's firm conviction is that the only answer to Britain's desperate situation is a heaven-sent Holy Spirit revival, but which may only come, as in the case of Joel chapter 2, when Britain is in such dire and desperate straits that she has to cry mightily to God for it.

The Trumpet Sounds For Britain is to be issued in a series of three volumes, of which this is Volume 1. The second volume will look at some of God's mighty acts of deliverance.

'Write the vision, and make it plain upon tables, that he may run that readeth it. For the vision is yet for an appointed time, but at the end it shall speak, and not lie: though it tarry, wait for it; because it will surely come, it will not tarry.'
Habakkuk 2:2,3

Chapter One
The Mighty Cleavage

Looking right back into the history of this country, there is every reason to say that it was due to an act of Almighty God that we ever became an island, or a group of islands – a fact which should not be allowed to go unmentioned in view of present-day developments.

For instance, not everybody will be aware that there was a period in our geological history when Britain was not an island; a period to which historians refer as 'pre-insular Britain'. At that time, this country was literally joined, in the geographical sense, to the continent of Europe and formed part of the European mainland. Therefore, when the very earliest prowling, primitive hunters came from Europe in those dim, distant days of our past, searching in our forests for the swine, reindeer and early mammoth which was their prey, they came *overland*. For the chalk downs of Dover were united in one long continuous range with the chalk cliffs of Calais, and there were no waters of the English Channel flowing in between. Furthermore, England and Holland were joined together by a wide marshy plain, and the Thames meandered majestically through it and merged into the lower Rhine.

Suddenly, a tremendous severance occurred. At some time in the far distant past, which experts on the subject say must have been even before the Pyramids were built, a violent earthquake caused an immense convulsion to take place in the region of the North Sea, and a great oceanic surge came sweeping round the northern coasts of Scotland and down towards the east coast of England. In the midst of this convulsion, the marshy plain sank a few hundred feet beneath the waves and thus admitted the mighty Atlantic Ocean to the North Sea and the Baltic. As a result, our islands were severed from the Continent at a point roughly between the Netherlands and what is now the coast of Norfolk and Suffolk; and today it is still the case that trawlers, whilst fishing off the Dogger Bank and over that part of the plain which now lies submerged under the North Sea, sometimes bring up in their nets the bones of mammoths or reindeer, and fragments of oak trees which tell their own tale.

Another violent earth tremor sundered the cliffs of Dover from the cliffs of Calais and Cap Gris Nez so that the Atlantic Ocean came surging through, gouging out with its strong tides what we now know as the English Channel. Ireland had already been cut adrift from England before the Dover Straits were pierced by the sea in this way, probably by a similar convulsion.

So Britain was constituted an island and a group of islands – for all time. Churchill, in the preface to his *History of the English-speaking Peoples*, says: 'No wanderings henceforth of little clans, in search of game or food-yielding plants, from the plains of France or Belgium, to the wooded valleys and downs of Southern England; no small ventures in dug-out canoes across narrow inlets at slack water. Those who come now must come in ships, and bold and wary they must be to face and master the Channel fogs and the Channel tides, and all that may lie beyond them.'

From then onwards, any would-be intruder into these islands would forever be confronted with this barrier of the sea, and would have those dangerous waters to cross.

And how often, since this mighty cleavage took place, have those twenty-five miles of water been the means of our national salvation!

They were, at the time of the Armada. They were again in Napoleon's day. And they were, more recently, immediately after the evacuation from Dunkirk and through the Battle of Britain.

I believe that this was all due to a mighty act of God. It was all part of God's plan; *God's* activity. How else do you explain that mighty under-water convulsion and the great act of severance, the result of which has played such a significant part in our history? What we need to understand above everything else is that at the back of all *visible* history is the *unseen* history – the thing that God is doing. I believe that what we see here, is the first of those great works which God has done for Britain. He had determined it all beforehand – even before creation and time began – and then he brought it to pass.

And there are strong biblical grounds for asserting this. For the Bible says that it is God who divided up the peoples of the world into nations, and who then divided to the nations their inheritance. Furthermore, it says that it is God who 'hath determined . . . the bounds of their habitation' – the borders of it, in other words. And the Bible gives the reason why: 'That they should seek the Lord, if haply they might feel after him and find him' (see Deuteronomy 32:7,8; Acts 17:26,27). Somehow or other, God's appointment of a nation's geographical position and boundaries – although it may be a mystery – is directly related to its people's, and maybe to other people's, eternal salvation.

For some reason known only to himself, when God Almighty was dividing to the nations their inheritances and setting the bounds of their habitations, he decreed that the people of this nation, – on whose behalf he was going to do so much – should dwell in a land that he himself had constituted an island.

Chapter Two
Christian Foundations

From all that we know, it is clear that the hand of God was at work at a very early stage in our history to ensure that this country was built on Christian foundations. In fact, the evidence shows that Christianity was here far earlier than most people realise.

I understand, for instance, that before Winston Churchill wrote his *History of the English-speaking Peoples* he employed an army of research workers, seeking to discover when it was that Christianity first came to these islands. They found their task was impossible. Christianity was already here when the first missionaries arrived.

It is quite wrong to think – as is popularly supposed – that everything began with Augustine, or with Augustine's particular branch of Christianity. This is most certainly not so. It is true that Augustine is frequently referred to as 'the Apostle of the English'. But Augustine did not arrive on these shores until the year AD 596, and Christianity had already been here long before that. It had probably been here over 500 years. And this means that it must have been a Christianity which was nearer to the pure New Testament form of Christianity than that which was brought here in AD 596.

Now it is most important to the theme of this book that

we look a little more closely into the matter. *When,* in fact, did Christianity first arrive here? *How* exactly did it come? And in what *form* did it come?

With regard to timing, it could have come direct from Pentecost, or very soon after, and I propose, a little further on, to give some good reasons why that could well have been the case.

This much can most certainly be established, that early Christianity in Britain dates at least as far back as the period of the Roman occupation of these islands, which can be dated quite definitely. Any history book will tell you that the Roman occupation of Britain began with the conquest of England by the Emperor Claudius who, incidentally, is the Claudius Caesar mentioned several times in the Acts of the Apostles (see, for instance, Acts 11:28; 18:2). That shows us how British history was running parallel with the events of the New Testament. It was in the year AD 43 that the Roman legions landed in Kent and, after several battles, achieved a decisive victory, with the result that Claudius returned to Rome from Britain with a long train of captives, and received from the Roman Senate the title of Emperor Britannicus.

From AD 43, therefore, Britannia became one of the forty-five provinces of the great Roman Empire, and remained so for four hundred years, until AD 407. That is a fact of history. No one can gainsay it.

The next thing which can be established is what the historians say of this period: 'The Roman occupation of Britain *gave time for the Christian faith to be planted.*' (my italics) Note that! It is very significant.

They also add that 'It was within that period that there arose a British Christian church which sent its bishops to the early councils.' This would seem to settle the matter pretty conclusively. Early Christianity would have had to be quite strongly established to be in a position to do that.

It is also of great interest to discover that G. M. Trevelyan, one of our most noted historians, places it on record that 'When the last of the Roman legions left these shores, and the Roman passed out of the story of Britain, they left behind them just three things of value, and the first of these was Welsh Christianity.'

I find that interesting, not only because it provides additional evidence to establish beyond any shadow of doubt that Christianity was already here well within this period of the Roman occupation, but also because Trevelyan's reference to 'Welsh' Christianity furnishes us with a clue as to what type of Christianity it was. The term 'Welsh' has a special significance in that respect, as we shall see a little later on.

Yet there are strong indications that Christianity was here even *earlier* than the period of the Roman occupation. And this is the point at which I shall examine the reasons why it could well have been here very soon after Pentecost.

First there is a need to put the entire subject into its proper context. What we are really talking about is not just the arrival of Christianity in Britain, but the arrival of Christianity in the world itself. And when we are considering the matter from that point of view, the most important thing to remember is that *God* planned it all. Indeed it is true to say that just as God had foreordained when and where his Son should come into the world to die for men's sins, so he had foreordained the ways by which the news concerning Jesus Christ should spread throughout the world, including just when it was to arrive in different places and countries, and by what means.

God had pre-arranged it all. He had designed it. He had drawn up the blue-print. And after our Lord had been crucified and had risen again, God began to put his predetermined plan into operation. Indeed he had been preparing the way long before the Saviour was born. And one of the means which he had purposed beforehand to put to his own use was the rise of the great Roman Empire which, when once Julius Caesar had planted its power firmly and widely on the north side of the Alps and into Gaul, stretched right across the world from East to West. And, in the providence of God, the roads which the Romans built across this great empire paved the way for the spread of the Gospel.

All the historians recognise the deep significance of this. For each in his turn gives testimony to the fact that 'The great Roman Empire, which arose after Julius Caesar, became the arena for the propagation of Christianity, which travelled to the four corners of civilisation in a very quick time by the roads built and guarded by the Roman soldiers.' And Churchill, when stressing this speedy means of communication, further enlarged upon the scene by telling us that 'The movement across this great Roman Empire was as rapid as when Queen Victoria came to the throne, and there were no obstructions of frontiers, laws, currency, or nationalism to hinder it.'

It needs to be repeated that, in all this, God was preparing the way, everywhere, for the arrival of Christianity.

In the context of all these developments which were taking place in the wider world at this time, something very significant began to happen *in Britain*.

Only a matter of fifty-five years before the birth of our Lord Jesus Christ in Bethlehem, Julius Caesar first landed in Britain, returning the following year. We are told that these two landings were but exploratory in nature; that they did not accomplish a great deal. What they *did* do, we are told, was to pave the way for the conquest of Britain under Claudius Caesar in AD 43.

However, I am intrigued to discover that the landings by Julius Caesar did something else besides pave the way for Britain's conquest under Claudius. They opened the way for the arrival of the Gospel. G. M. Trevelyan records that from the time of Julius Caesar's departure from these shores, a peaceful penetration of Britain by travellers from Rome and from other and more distant

parts of the Roman Empire began (including all the Mediterranean countries), and continued throughout this
interval of one hundred years between Julius Caesar's
departure from Britain and the conquest by Claudius. All
of which is very significant to our theme.

Why do I say this? The answer becomes apparent when
we place the arrival and beginnings of Christianity in their
historical setting. Christianity is based on fact – *historical*
fact – a point which, in my own opinion, has not been
stressed anywhere near sufficiently in past days, and is
one which needs to be emphasised more and more today.

All the major events concerning its beginnings can be
placed within a specific time-scale, including those which
began to take place in the Roman province of Judea
round about this time. We have already seen how God
had been preparing the way beforehand for the spread of
the Christian message. But, of course, it follows that
before Christianity itself could be spread, the Saviour of
the world had to come.

So we read: 'But when the fulness of the time was come,
God sent forth his Son' (Galatians 4:4). This means that
when everything was ready, when the way had been fully
prepared, when the world scene had been well and truly
set, when certain figures such as Pontius Pilate and
Caiaphas were already on the stage – then God sent his
Son. And he did this just fifty-four years after Julius
Caesar's second landing in Britain.

Luke in his Gospel places this great event in its precise
historical setting by telling us that the birth of our Lord
Jesus Christ took place at Bethlehem in the days of the
Roman emperor, Caesar Augustus – an historical figure.
He was emperor from 31 BC to AD 14, and the birth of
Jesus Christ took place during this time. You will remember the familiar words: 'And it came to pass in those days,
that there went out a decree from Caesar Augustus, that
all the world should be taxed.' (Luke 2:1)

To pin-point the time still further, Luke goes on to say

that 'This taxing was first made when Cyrenius was governor of Syria.' (Luke 2:2) Cyrenius was another historical figure. Everybody living in the region of Palestine in those days knew him. It is rather like saying that such-and-such an event took place when Sir Winston Churchill was prime minister of Great Britain, or when George VI was king of England.

This places the event in its historical setting, and within a definite time-scale. Luke does this kind of thing again when he begins to relate the arrival on the scene of John the Baptist at the beginning of his public ministry. 'Now in the fifteenth year of the reign of Tiberius Caesar, Pontius Pilate being governor of Judea, and Herod being tetrarch of Galilee . . . Annas and Caiaphas being the high priests, the word of God came unto John the son of Zacharius in the wilderness.' (Luke 3:1–2)

There they all are. The historical figures – well-known figures – who were on the world scene at that time.

Christianity is based on *fact*. All the main events relating to its beginning can be placed against this specific time-scale. Caesar Augustus, who had been emperor of Rome at the time of the Saviour's birth, was succeeded by Tiberius Caesar. He reigned as emperor from AD 14 to AD 37. That is a fact. And to place the arrival of John the Baptist in its historical setting, as he came to prepare the way for our Lord's public ministry, Luke tells us that it was in the fifteenth year of Tiberius Caesar's emperorship.

Luke (3:1) even tells us who was in charge of the other regions of Palestine at this time. Philip, Herod's brother, was tetrarch of Iturea and of the region of Trachonitis and Lysanias was 'tetrarch of Abilene'. Both were well-known figures.

Then we read in this same third chapter of Luke's Gospel that our Lord began his earthly ministry when he was about thirty years of age (see Luke 3:23). We know that his crucifixion and resurrection took place three years later, followed, forty days after that, by his ascen-

sion into heaven, from whence he poured forth his Holy
Spirit upon the original 120 disciples on the Day of
Pentecost. And thus were the disciples empowered to
take the Gospel throughout the world – beginning at
Jerusalem.

What we are able to see from a review of this time-scale
is that all the main events in our Saviour's life took place
within the two historical points of Roman and British
history to which we have referred earlier, namely, the
landings in Britain by Julius Caesar on the one hand, and
the invasion of Britain by the Emperor Claudius on the
other. We also know that there were a few years to spare
on either side.

So we can understand that if we place the crucifixion of
our blessed Lord in the year AD 33, the gap in years
between the world-shaking event on the Day of Pentecost
and Claudius Caesar's invasion of Britain was very
narrow indeed. Just a matter of ten years, in fact.

Why do I get so excited about all this?

Why, because from the point of view of discovering
when Christianity first arrived in this country, I find it
very exciting indeed to find that the historian Trevelyan
has this to say about all these things: 'The hundred most
important years in the history of the world' (note that
perceptive phrase: it is an historian, not a theologian, who
is using it) – 'The hundred most important years in the
history of the world were not wholly blank, *even in
Britain.*' (my italics)

A most significant statement indeed. What did he mean
by it?

Well, he goes on to explain, by revealing what was
happening in Britain within those vital and very crucial
one hundred years. 'While Julius Caesar was being mur-
dered and avenged, while the loves of Antony and
Cleopatra were raising the question of the relation of East
and West inside the Roman world, while Jesus Christ was
preaching and while Paul was being converted – through-

out all this period, far in the north, Roman traders and colonists, working from the base of the Romanised province of Gaul, were *establishing settlements in the interior of Britain* and gaining influence at the courts of its tribal kings.' (my italics)

You notice what he is telling us. They were doing this whilst all these things were happening within the Roman Empire. They were doing it *while Jesus Christ was preaching* and while Paul was being converted – establishing settlements in the interior of Britain. Roman traders and colonists were doing that, while Caesar Augustus was busy constructing the empire – the Caesar Augustus who features in the Bethlehem story.

This means that the Romans were establishing settlements in Britain even before Jesus Christ was born; on, after that, through the time of his childhood, earthly ministry, crucifixion and resurrection, up to Pentecost and beyond. Merchants and traders were travelling backwards and forwards between the Mediterranean countries and coming, with merchandise and produce, right into the interior of Britain, to the settlements which they had established there.

That is what I meant by saying that while all these other developments, such as the construction of roads, were taking place in the wider world and in the Middle-Eastern countries, something very significant and directly related to our theme began to happen in Britain. For I see in this the finger of God at work, preparing the way for an early arrival of the Gospel – a *very* early arrival of that Gospel. It was all happening according to the predeterminate counsel and foreknowledge of God.

Immediately Julius Caesar had landed in Britain, he had extended the trade routes from the Roman province of Gaul across to this country. Some fifty-five years before our Lord was born at Bethlehem, a way had begun to be opened up for any news about Jesus of Nazareth and the mighty miracles which he wrought – if not yet his teaching – to be carried, when the time was ready, from the Mediterranean, right across the Roman world via the trade routes into Britain. And the time between our Lord's birth and the beginning of his public ministry would have given a further thirty years for that route to be established by ever-increasing use. Altogether, there is a period of some eighty-five years involved.

This was God at work. When Gaius Julius Caesar, the proconsul of Gaul, first fixed his eyes upon Britain in the summer of 55 BC, he was about to accomplish more than he knew. Maybe in human eyes he was preparing the way for the later Roman conquest. But under the overruling providence of God he was preparing the way for the early arrival of Christianity. And in that sense he was God's instrument, although he would have been completely unaware of that fact.

The more I think and ponder about these things, the more I am persuaded that there is no reason whatsoever why faith in Christ, in terms of a personal belief in him, could not have been brought to Britain direct from Pentecost, or at least very soon after it. A study of history would seem to indicate that God was working to that end.

I am particularly convinced of this when I remember that there were gathered together in Jerusalem for the Feast of Pentecost, 'Jews, devout men, out of every nation under heaven.' (Acts 2:5) They could easily have included people from those settlements in Britain, especially if we are meant to take that phrase 'out of every nation under heaven' literally. For every nation under heaven included Britain.

And then, what happened? The Holy Spirit came down in tongues of fire upon the original disciples of Jesus. He was poured down upon them from heaven by the now enthroned Lord Jesus. Then this great multitude of devout Jews, who had come from so many nations, rushed together in the streets of Jerusalem to see what had happened. The disciples went out to them and Peter preached his first sermon. As a result 3,000 of them were converted to Jesus

Christ; then 5,000; and then a little later on, very many more.

But wait! What transpired when the Feast of Pentecost was over? Those who had arrived in Jerusalem from all these countries, returned to the various nations from which they had come; and when they did so, thousands who had been converted to Jesus Christ took their new-found faith with them – the Christian faith. Remember that it was no mere verbal belief or creed, not just a written formula or set of beliefs. These men went back *indwelt by the Spirit of Jesus Christ.* It is important to realise this, because it is what being converted to Jesus Christ really means; what makes a man a Christian. And if any of them had indeed come from Britain, they returned to Britain carrying the Spirit of the Lord within them.

In any case, in view of the numbers involved in these early Jerusalem conversions (there were not just hundreds of them, but thousands), some of them must have been merchants and traders who, in pursuit of their occupation, spent much of their time travelling backwards and forwards across the Roman world. It is quite inconceivable that this was not the case. After all, they were Jews! And for many of them, merchandise and trading was their means of livelihood, and travelling the caravan routes their very way of life. After the Feast of Pentecost was over, they would have continued to travel with their goods. But now they were new creatures in Christ Jesus, filled with the joy of the new life which they would have wanted to share with others. Because they had been so filled with the Holy Spirit, these people would surely have taken the Gospel wherever they went, to be discussed and talked about. And so faith in Christ Jesus would be carried very far afield. No doubt there was amongst them, too, the kind of trader who travelled backwards and forwards between the Mediterranean countries and the West, as far as those settlements in the very interior of Britain.

We need also to remember that many of those devout

people who had converged on Jerusalem for the festival had not come on their own. They had come in families and in groups – the Jew is noted for his family links. When they returned, they returned in families and in groups – but now, in many cases, as *Christian* groups. When they got back home, they used these Christian groups as nucleii for establishing Christian churches in the various countries, towns and cities from whence they had come. These cities and towns were situated all along the main highways and trade routes throughout the provinces of the Roman Empire, and that is one of the explanations why Christianity spread so quickly. This was God at work. There was a divine strategy involved at Pentecost, and here we see part of it in operation. God did not have to wait for 'missionaries', as we call them, to go into the various countries of the world and take the message of Christianity with them. Indeed, he did not do so. He brought together this great multitude 'out of every nation under heaven' and then, initially, used *them* to go back to their countries and provinces to plant Christian churches or groups of believers there. They were the forerunners, so to speak, which possibly explains why it was that when the apostle Paul came to Ephesus on his third missionary journey he found that there was already a nucleus of believers in that city (Acts 19:1,7). It may also explain the existence of a Christian church at a very early stage as far west as Rome.

We know that a group of Christians was already there during the time of Claudius Caesar (AD 41-54). For while the apostle Paul was in Corinth on his second missionary journey, he met Aquila and Priscilla who, we are told in Acts 18:2, had 'lately come from Italy . . . because that *Claudius* had commanded all Jews to depart from Rome'. Roman historians inform us that this expulsion was due to riots and disputes which had been levelled against the Christians by the Jewish communities, especially over the one who was called Christus or 'the Christ'.

A study of the Acts and one of the epistles makes it plain that the community of believers in Rome had already been in existence a number of years by the time the apostle Paul had completed his third missionary journey in the spring of AD 57. Whilst he was on that journey, Paul wrote to the Christians in Rome, telling them in advance that it was his intention to visit them shortly, on his way to Spain. The very existence of Paul's epistle to the Romans is evidence enough for the existence of this Christian community at an early stage. But in that letter he says that he had had a great desire 'these many years to come unto you' (see Romans 15:22-29), a statement which in itself proves that this group of believers in Rome had already been in existence a number of years.

It was not only 'in existence'. It was a very strong and influential Christian community at this early stage, for in his letter the apostle says: 'I thank my God through Jesus Christ *for you all,* that your faith is spoken of throughout the whole world.' (Romans 1:8) In other words, this group of believers was acting as a kind of 'sounding board' from which faith in Christ – their faith – was somehow or other being heard about, and indeed spoken of all over the Roman Empire. This, too, was God at work. The approximate time when this letter to the believers in Rome was written was AD 56, and Britain had already been a province of the Roman Empire for twelve years. So no doubt the faith of these Christians in Rome was being discussed at that time in Britain also. Do we now begin to see the significance of the statement regarding Winston Churchill's research workers? They had found it impossible to discover when it was that Christianity first came to Britain, because it was already here when the first missionaries arrived.

There is something very significant to learn from those early missionary journeys. The church at Antioch had been established well over a year before Claudius

Caesar's conquest of Britain. That is made plain from a reading of Acts 11:19-30 and by comparing relative dates. Paul then used Antioch as the base from which he set out on his missionary journeys. In fact, it was the Holy Spirit who sent him out from there (Acts 13:2-4).

A study of what followed, from the Acts of the Apostles, reveals that during his *second* missionary journey, when Paul and his party would have turned southwards, 'they were forbidden of the Holy Ghost to preach the word in Asia'; when they were intending to turn eastwards, again 'the Spirit suffered them not' (see Acts 16:6-8). From the remainder of Acts we read that thereafter the Gospel was brought *westwards* – ever westwards. I find that very significant, and particularly when it is very apparent that this movement westwards was all under the Holy Spirit's control. By AD 60, very much under the direction of the Lord himself, Paul had arrived at Rome, where he preached for two years (Acts 28:16-31).

It was his intention, as we have already seen, to go on as far as Spain. Indeed, some authorities claim that he was released from open imprisonment after those two years in Rome, and that between then and the time when he was martyred for his faith, he fulfilled his intention of taking the Gospel as far west as Spain. If that is indeed true, the Gospel could very quickly have reached Britain from Spain, either by the sea-route across the Bay of Biscay and round the coast of France, or overland through the Roman province of Gaul, and thence across the Channel to this country.

There were many ways by which the Gospel was being carried westwards along the roads which, by the providence of God, had been prepared beforehand. All that I have said so far does not even take into account the fact that, when persecution arose against the Christians in Jerusalem after the martyrdom of Stephen, 'they that were scattered abroad went everywhere preaching the word' (Acts 8:4) and, as later chapters reveal, planted churches wherever they went. Neither does it take into account that, when once Paul had planted churches along the trade routes of the eastern Mediterranean, he was able to say of more than one of them: 'From you sounded out the word of the Lord not only in Macedonia and Achaia, but also in every place your faith to God-ward is spread abroad; so that we need not to speak anything.' (1 Thessalonians 1:8) This was the amazing characteristic of the Thessalonian church; it was also the mark of the early Christians in Rome, not to mention many other Christian churches in those early days. In addition to all this, we have the evidence of the historian Eusebius (AD 260-340) who states that 'The apostles passed beyond the ocean to the isles called the Britannic Isles.'

The more I consider all this and dwell on the implications involved, the more I am led to believe that there is a strong case for saying that under the controlling influence and overruling direction of an Almighty God, Christianity could have arrived in Britain very early. All the evidence points that way. Whatever may be the truth concerning *how* it arrived, the facts, when taken together, point to an early arrival, not a late one. And some of the facts suggest that it *could* have arrived during the ten-year interval between Pentecost and Claudius Caesar's conquest, before Britain became a Roman province, and perhaps not very long after the Day of Pentecost. Those facts certainly suggest that Christianity came to Britain in apostolic times.

Or put it this way: I believe it is true to say that the Son of Righteousness had not long arisen from his grave on the day of his resurrection and ascended into the heavens, before the first transforming beams of his re-creative light began to penetrate the heathen darkness of some hearts in our islands.

The main reason for pursuing this theme is that it helps to establish the *type* of Christianity which was first brought to Britain. For if it came direct from Pentecost, or even twenty to thirty years after Pentecost, there is no doubt that it would have been the original New Testament form of Christianity, or something very closely akin to it.

After all, we know what type of Christianity was held by that original group of believers in Rome. We have only to read the sixteen chapters of Paul's epistle to the Romans to find out! For the purpose of that letter was to get them thoroughly grounded in the essentials of the Christian faith. And Paul leaves us in no doubt that it was original, genuine Christianity that he was teaching, and of the purest kind, because he makes it plain in his epistle to the Galatians that he received it direct from the Lord Jesus himself: 'I certify you, brethren, that the gospel which was preached of me is not after man. For I neither received it of man, neither was I taught it, but by the revelation of Jesus Christ.' (Galatians 1:11,12) He also made it plain that there were terrible consequences for preaching anything else. 'Though we, or an angel from heaven, preach any other gospel unto you than that which we have preached unto you, let him be accursed. . . . so say I now again, if any man preach any other gospel unto you than that ye have received, let him be accursed.' (Galatians 1:8,9)

It was *this* type of Christianity – received direct from the Lord himself – which all the apostles proclaimed and which was held in Rome by these early Christians between the years AD 60 and 62 when the apostle Paul was there preaching it. It was this type of Christianity which was being 'sounded forth' throughout the whole of the Mediterranean world. It was this type of Christianity which became embodied in the epistles and Gospels. And it would have been this type of Christianity which was carried to Britain, if the speed of travel in those days made it possible for it to arrive here at a very early date.

The fact of the matter is that it arrived! God had planned that it should, and had been preparing the way for its arrival from the time of Julius Caesar. And Christianity was definitely well established here at least as early as the Roman occupation in AD 43 – only ten years after Pentecost.

So God was at work very early in our history to ensure that these islands were well and truly built on Christian foundations. He must have had a very good reason for doing this.

Chapter Three

Three Great Landmarks

A study of the first one thousand years or so of British history will show that God so caused the Christianity which he had placed here to spread and grow, that under his guiding hand we were brought to three great landmarks.

First, a good two hundred years before the reign of King Alfred, God brought us to that point when, to quote the words of Winston Churchill: 'There was no kingdom in the realm in which *heathen* religions and practices now prevailed. The whole Island was now Christian.'

Here is a very significant statement which, in the light of what we see happening in our country today, confronts us with a tremendous challenge. It means that the island – which before the birth of our Lord Jesus Christ, and long before the days of Julius Caesar, had been the chief centre of ancient Druid worship; to which people from many a far-off land had come to receive instruction about this cult and to learn its dreadful heathen practices; where, in those days, human sacrifices were being made, and where human blood was being offered on heathen altars; where, later, temples to Mithras had been erected, and where, still later, the ancient gods of Thor and Woden held considerable sway – *that* island had so rallied to the Christian faith, that the great Venerable Bede was able to give this description of it: 'A Christian England . . . divided into seven kingdoms of varying strength, all professing the Gospel of Christ.'

It shows that God was so causing Christianity to grow, that all the regions and kingdoms in England which were under the sway of these heathen gods and practices had gradually, but perceptibly, submitted to the Lordship of Jesus Christ.

This is both an inspiring example and a clear demonstration of how certain statements of Scripture about the enthronement in heaven of our ascended Lord Jesus were being worked out in Britain at that time – such passages as those which say that God has 'raised him from the dead, and set him at his own right hand in the heavenly places, far above all principality, and power, and might, and dominion . . . and hath put all things under his feet . . . Sit on my right hand, until I make thine enemies thy footstool . . . For he must reign till he hath put all enemies under his feet.' (Ephesians 1:20-22; Hebrews 1:13; 1 Corinthians 15:25)

It is one of the glories of the Christian Gospel that all contestants, rival powers, gods and religions must, and will, be brought into subjection under the Lord Jesus Christ. As Christianity began to spread and grow, we see that truth being worked out in Britain on quite a considerable scale. Nobody can say that it was not God who was doing this, for whoever might have been the human instruments at the time, the Scriptures make it abundantly plain that one man plants and another waters, but it is *God* who gives the increase (1 Corinthians 3:6).

Then secondly, God brought us to that point during the twelfth century where – and I quote Winston Churchill again – 'After . . . years of being the encampment and battleground of an invading army, England became finally and for all time one coherent kingdom based on Christianity.'

This was at the time of Henry Plantagenet (Henry II,

1154-1189). We had reached another significant peak in our history which testifies to the fact that Christian growth and development has so continued under God that, by the time the British Isles had become *one* kingdom out of many kingdoms, the foundation of that one kingdom was the foundation of Christianity.

It was the rock on which the island kingdom had been built. You will notice that Churchill does not just say 'one coherent kingdom' but was at pains to stress that it was 'one coherent kingdom based on Christianity'.

'Finally and for all time', he wrote in a book first published in 1956 – a mere quarter of a century ago! For so he thought.

A united kingdom based on Christianity was a position which became so firmly established in the nation that eventually it became the position *constitutionally*.

This brings me to the *third* great landmark to which God Almighty brought us. The Christian faith – and here I need to stress that it was the *Protestant* Christian faith – became Britain's constitutional basis to such an extent that it was embodied by an act of Parliament in the Coronation Oath.

Many people will argue that our British Constitution is an unwritten one. The truth of the matter is that we have a *written* part of that constitution, and the written part happens to be Christian. It is, I repeat, embodied by Act of Parliament in the Coronation Oath. This still requires each Sovereign 'to uphold, to the utmost of my power, the Laws of God in the Realm; and the True Profession of the Christian Gospel.' The Sovereign, with a hand upon an open Bible, is on oath before Almighty God to do that, and Parliament pledges itself in the Coronation Service, through its senior peers, to support him or her. The position could not have been made more strong.

I need to emphasise this last point, because when the Christian position was embodied by Act of Parliament in the British Constitution, it made – or should have made –

those Christian foundations secure. Evidence abounds that Almighty God has been at work all down the years of our history to ensure that this nation was built on Christian foundations, and that the nation was to be governed by the laws of God, even to the point of ensuring that the Christian position became the British position constitutionally.

Chapter Four

Through Spiritual Darkness

There is overwhelming evidence to show that whenever those foundations have been in danger, either of being destroyed or of being eroded and gradually whittled away, God has been at work to ensure that they were either strengthened and buttressed or, where necessary, totally restored. We shall consider just a few of the outstanding examples.

It was true at the time of St Patrick, when this country was passing through one of its very early periods of great darkness.

The Christianity which God had so graciously brought to these islands so early, was taking root and spreading during the period of the Roman occupation of Britain to such an extent that Churchill, thrilled with excitement and caught up with the spirit of its onward march, proclaims with great exuberance: 'The new creed was winning victories everywhere.'

Then, at just about the time when Roman civilisation in this country was reaching its highest peak, a terrible and devasting menace of unprecedented proportions began to shake and convulse the nation. In the north, the Scots from Ireland and the Picts from Scotland were ferociously assaulting the defences of Hadrian's Wall, whilst at the same time the Saxons from Europe rowed across the

36

North Sea in their long boats and heavily attacked the east coast all the way from Dover to Newcastle. Thus, whilst the Romans were still in occupation, the inroads of these barbarian peoples began.

In the year 367, the Picts and the Scots and the Saxons all seemed to work in combination with one another, for all fell together on Britannia and circumstances of supreme and murderous horror beset our island. At that time also, the Roman Empire itself was being assailed by invading hordes, and was obliged to withdraw the legions from these shores in an attempt to defend the more immediate borders.

Less than forty years after the last of these legions had departed, in the year 442, there was added to the already devastating forces of the Saxons, Picts, and Scots, a mass migration of assaulting barbarians coming from north Germany across the North Sea to Britain. A period of terrible carnage and destruction began, and from this time onwards the curtains closed down on our history. The period called the Dark Ages had been ushered in, and a long, dark night fell upon Britannia.

What happened behind those curtains throughout these years is impossible to tell, for the darkness which closed in was so terrible that almost all records of events were completely obliterated, and the invaders kept none. Hence the next two hundred years of our history are left almost entirely blank. When those curtains lifted again it was revealed that an entire civilisation had been wiped out. The dawn broke on a scene of terrible devastation.

The well-planned Roman cities with their defensive walls had all been levelled to the ground with powerful battering rams. In place of the strong Roman-built stone houses, equipped with central-heating, baths, and many another 'modern' facility, there now stood only the wooden huts of the more primitive barbarians. All around, the roofless shells of Roman cities and villas stood starkly on the horizons. Their ruins were sprinkled over the entire land. Trevelyan says it is impossible to exaggerate in any way the injury which had been done to Roman-British civilisation in this two-century interval.

Our country was desolate; our towns and cities had been burned with fire. Strangers had devoured and overthrown it in our presence. A complete way of life had perished, with all its culture. Four hundred years of law, order, craftsmanship, science and learning had been ruthlessly swept away. The people had even lost the art of writing. Confusion and conflict reigned everywhere. As he surveys the appalling scene which emerged, Churchill laments: 'England was once again a barbarian island. It had been Christian, it was now heathen.'

It would seem, from such a grim description, that all lights had been entirely put out. Yet despite all that had happened, there was outstanding evidence that God had kept his hand on our history throughout the whole of this period, to retain our Christian foundations even in the midst of this great darkness.

In the first place, he had preserved and nurtured more than a remnant of that already existing Christian church. For in the face of the terrible barbarian onslaught, the British church had fallen back with other survivors upon the western parts of the island, and had taken refuge behind the Welsh mountains. There, under the hand of God, it continued to be spiritually fed, nurtured and encouraged, throughout this dark period, by Christian missionaries who kept coming over from the Continent to ensure that faith was sustained. It was a miracle of divine preservation.

It can be likened to the time of which Emperor Haile Selassie of Ethiopia spoke when he was last in Europe – the time when his early forefathers, on seeing how the onrush of Islam threatened to engulf the churches of the Middle East and so extinguish the light of the Gospel, determined that Ethiopia, surrounded as she was by her mountain ranges, should remain an island site for the preservation of Christianity in the Middle East.

Something very similar happened here, preserving Christianity in the British Isles during the period of these barbarian invasions. As one historian has put it: 'There, far to the West, whilst the rest of Britain was being ravaged and shaken by these ferocious hordes – cut off from the rest of the world by the barbarian flood, but defended by its mountains – there remained this tiny Christian realm.'

I find it tremendously inspiring to think about this. Christians often sing:

> Crowns and thrones may perish,
> Kingdoms rise and wane,
> But the Church of Jesus
> Constant will remain.

> Gates of Hell can never
> 'Gainst that Church prevail,
> We have Christ's own promise
> And that cannot fail.

These lines are based on our Lord's own words: 'Upon this rock I will build my church; and the gates of hell shall not prevail against it.' Here, during the Dark Ages, is an outstanding example of his words being marvellously fulfilled.

It is also one of the occasions in history where we see meaning being given to some well-known words in Hebrews 12:26-27, and in quite a remarkable way. God says: 'Yet once more, I shake not the earth only, but also heaven. And this word...', says the writer of the epistle, 'signifieth the removing of those things that are shaken, as of things that are made, that those things which cannot be shaken may remain.' Which is exactly what happened.

If any preacher or Bible-class leader wants a living example to illustrate and explain what those words from the epistle to the Hebrews mean, he certainly has one here. For Britain was being violently shaken throughout

the whole of this two-hundred-year period, and during
that shaking there was a removal of the things that are
made by man. Walled cities, well-built Roman villas,
works of art, craftsmanship, an entire culture – all were
swept away and became obliterated. Yet there was one
thing that remained: the church of Jesus Christ. *That*
could not be shaken. It proved indestructible. It remained
intact.

Hebrews 12:28 goes on to say of Christians: 'Wherefore
we receiving a kingdom which cannot be moved'. When
Christians who were living at the time when this terrible
period of darkness had ended, saw how all else around
them had perished, those words must have had a profound effect upon them. And when we, who may well be
called to pass through a similar time of darkness, realise
the full force of the words in the context of all that
happened in those dark days, they should have a profound effect upon us too.

The preservation of the Christian church, then, was *one*
of the miracles which God wrought during this period.
History also reveals that God in his infinite goodness also
used this very darkness to do a work of consolidation. For
historians show how, all through this day of trouble, the
Christian faith – which was driven back behind the Welsh
mountains – got such a hold over the Welsh, that by the
fifth and sixth centuries they had come to regard Christianity as their distinguishing mark.

Almighty God was not only at work to ensure that
Christianity was nurtured and preserved all through this
long period. He was also at work to ensure that Christianity should once again be spread. We know this
because, as is so often the case in such a time, his eyes were
already upon a man. God usually works through *people*;
and certainly when he is purposing to turn the tide of
darkness.

The terrible time of trouble had not long begun, when a
band of raiders from Ireland came across to the Severn

valley, carried away captive a lad by the name of Patrick, the son of a Christian deacon, and sold him into slavery when they got back to Ireland. For six years he was obliged to tend and look after swine. But all this was of God: the hand of the Lord was upon him there, and during his long period of loneliness he was converted to Jesus Christ. He then received supernatural guidance that he should make his escape, which he did, and on reaching the coast managed to persuade a captain to take him on board his ship. After many wanderings, he found his way to some islands off Marseilles. His conversion must have been genuine, for during this time there began to well up within him an increasingly strong desire to go to his former captors in Ireland and return good for evil by sharing with them the good news of the Gospel. The guiding hand of God continued to rest upon him, for he came under the care of Bishop Germanus of Auxerre and, after fourteen years of preparation and training, sailed back to Ireland in 432.

By this time, the darkness was fast closing in over England. Just ten years later, the mass migration of barbarians from north Germany began. Britannia was plunged into night. These sombre words of Winston Churchill were uttered about that scene: 'Far away in the centre of the world where Christianity had had its origin, men remembered that Britain had been Christian once, and might be Christian again.'

But God had not been caught napping, not in any sense. He sees the end from the beginning, and even before the darkness finally fell, he had been preparing his instrument.

When the waves of barbarian Saxons from the Continent began to swarm over the east coast of England – to be followed in 442 by the migration from north Germany – Ireland, in the providence of God, was miraculously spared, and did not suffer any of these onslaughts. (The barbarians who had come from Ireland to the Severn valley and captured Patrick were the native Scots from Ireland, not continental invaders.) So God's eyes had not only been fixed upon a man; they had also been fixed upon a country. This was the country from which, in the great plan and purposes of God, Christianity was once again to be spread in the now darkened England.

Of God's chosen instrument who stepped back on the scene in Ireland just ten years before the curtain finally fell over England, we read: 'Then came Patrick, and gathered together those Christians that remained, and through them, proceeded to convert whole regions of Ireland to Jesus Christ.' It was out of Ireland, then – when Patrick's work of establishing churches there had been accomplished – that the light of Christianity began to shine once more like a gleaming beacon upon Britain. But only, as yet, *upon* it.

From Ireland, the Gospel was carried over to the northern part of Britain by Columba. When God's hour of deliverance for Britain had come, this Columba, imbued with the same fire and evangelistic zeal as Patrick, set up his group of beehive huts on the island of Iona. In 563, and using Iona as his base, he led swarms of missionaries over western Scotland and northern Britain. An ardent and vital movement of Christianity was therefore set afoot in the north, which spread quickly to the kingdom of Northumbria in the east and the British kingdom of Strathclyde in the west. Columba became the founder of the Scottish Christian church.

In this way, therefore, the message which Patrick had carried back to Ireland and had then proclaimed and caused to be well established there, came across the sea to these shores, and then spread widely through much of the northern regions, dispelling the darkness everywhere.

And all this was still before the arrival of Augustine. He was not to come for another thirty-three years! Indeed, in the light of what we have seen in a previous chapter about the early arrival of Christianity in Britain, it is important to stress at this point that the history books do not refer to the time of Patrick and Columba as the *coming* of Christianity to Britain; rather, they refer to it as the *return* of Christianity to Britain.

It is important also to note at this point that there was a distinction between the form of Christianity which reached England through Columba, and that form of Christianity which, by then, existed throughout the Christianised countries of Europe.

Equally important is the fact that it is *historians* who tell us (and they have no particular axe to grind) that the form of Christianity which Columba brought, had travelled from its original source in the Middle East, through Northern Ireland, to its new home in Scotland and the north of England *without touching at any moment the centre at Rome*.

It was not until Pope Gregory the Great sent Augustine as a missionary in 596, that the Roman form of Christianity which had come to dominate Western Europe was introduced to Britain. Thereafter, two streams of Christianity flowed through the land: the one which had been brought by Columba, and the Roman form which had come with Augustine. As time went on, the latter sought to exercise a position of supremacy over the former.

*   *   *   *

The time of King Alfred was another period when this country's Christian foundations were placed in great danger. We shall have cause to return, in Volume 2, to some of the great miracles of deliverance which God wrought on behalf of King Alfred when this country was being overrun by the Vikings.

How many people realise, however, that Alfred exerted a great Christian influence throughout the whole of his reign with lasting effect throughout these islands? Everybody has heard about King Alfred burning the cakes! But how many know that he said: 'There is only one way by which to build any kingdom, and that is on the sure and certain foundation of faith in Jesus Christ, and in Jesus Christ crucified, and it is on *that foundation* that I intend to build *my* kingdom'?

How many understand, too, with what great resolution and determination he sought to do this, as soon as God had given him final victory over the Vikings? He so painstakingly laid Christian foundations, that the effect of them has lasted to this day.

Chapter Five
The Reformation

We move now to the period of the English Reformation. This was certainly a time when the nation's Christian foundations were wonderfully restored, because the Reformation occurred when Britain was once again going through a period of intense spiritual darkness.

As we have already seen, the form of Christianity which came to Britain from Ireland had travelled with Patrick from its source in the eastern Mediterranean without reference to Rome. It is this which became known as 'Irish' or 'Celtic' Christianity, and in order to understand what happened subsequently, we need to look at the background more closely.

Under Patrick's leadership, this Celtic Christianity had taken the form of loosely-knit communities of devout Christians who separated themselves from the rest of mankind and lived in beehive huts made of wattle, clay, and turf, the huts often being grouped together in a fortified village or kraal under the supervision of an outstanding Christian leader on some rocky mountain or remote island.

The purpose of this separation was to so build themselves up in the faith that they could go out and convert whole areas and regions to Jesus Christ. These Christian communities were, by nature, missionary bases, and, in essence, this form of Christianity was independent. It was free from outside control. It was not, in this early period, associated in any way with the universal organisation of the papacy.

The devout life which these Christians lived, caused this Irish or Celtic form of Christianity to produce a rich crop of saints, of whom perhaps the greatest and most typical was Columba. He was born half a century after St Patrick's death and, was an offspring of his church. He founded his cluster of beehive huts on the small island of Iona off the west coast of Scotland round about 563, and from there, his missionaries had come over to northern Britain.

Now the papacy, from a very early stage, had followed with deep interest the results of St Columba's labour in Scotland and the north of England. It had seen, with thankfulness, that this was an ardent and zealous Christian movement which was breaking out in the northern parts of the far-off islands of Britain, and one which was full of fervour. Rome was also excited about the spread of the Gospel there. But she became deeply disturbed because the faith seemed to have been separately planted. She viewed with deep concern the fact that, from the very outset, it was independent of the papal throne.

Pope Gregory was the true founder of the medieval papacy and was the first of the great popes. These were the days when it was the first care of the Bishop of Rome to see that all Christians in every country should be brought under one earthly head. Therefore Gregory, and the ecclesiastical statesmen who were at that time gathered together in Rome, had sent Augustine to England in 596, not only to spread the Gospel in England further, but also to bring about an effective union between British Christians and what, in the Roman view, was the main body of the church.

Following the conversion of King Ethelbert of Kent, and after he had founded the see of Canterbury and made it the solid base for the subsequent spread of Roman Christianity over this island, Augustine set about this other task of bringing about the desired union of British Christians with Rome. From the outset, his attention became focused in a westerly direction, for his first attempt was directed towards the British church which, during the barbarian invasions, had been so miraculously preserved behind the Welsh mountains.

He summoned a conference of its British Christian bishops and Welsh representatives at the mouth of the river Severn. But the British bishops were in no mood for throwing themselves into the strong embraces of Rome. When Augustine claimed to have supremacy over all Christians in Britain by virtue of his Roman commission, they adamantly rejected his claim. They had defended the faith for so long against all the terrible cruelties and oppressions which the barbarians had levelled at them, and had remained independent, so why should they now subject themselves to being controlled from overseas? When Augustine threatened that if they did not submit, the Saxon armies in England would be used to bring the whole influence and prestige of Rome against them, they saw Rome in its true light.(It was one of the earliest indications that she intended to get what she wanted by force of arms if necessary.) That finished the matter as far as the British bishops and Welsh representatives were concerned, and the conference broke up in enmity. Augustine's attempt to bring about a union had totally failed and, with it, Rome's very first step in the direction of making Britain a Roman Catholic country. All further efforts by Augustine were virulently repulsed.

A second attempt was made by Rome more than half a century later, and this one was far more successful. It was levelled at the Celtic Christian missionaries operating in the north.

Once again Rome had become disturbed by the success of an ardent, evangelistic type of Christianity which was working independently of her. This time the leader was Aidan, Columba's successor. Aidan had founded the monastry of Melrose in east Scotland, and from there the surrounding districts of East, West, and Mid-Lothian beyond Northumbria were evangelised. The monastry of Lindisfarne on Holy Island off the Northumbrian and Lothian coast was also founded and Aidan became head of the Christian missionary community there. Then, at the invitation of King Oswald, Aidan began a mission to Oswald's kingdom of Northumbria in 635. This mission proved very successful. Indeed, strong bands of Celtic missionaries, under Aidan's dynamic leadership, not only reconverted Northumbria (which had relapsed) to the Christian faith, and not only evangelised the kingdom of Mercia which was just to the south, but they also continued in a southerly direction, penetrating to the south-east coast and bringing back East Anglia and Essex to Christianity. In fact, some of these Irish Christians even established groups of their missionary beehive huts as far south as Sussex, which was still heathen. They were winning victories wherever they went.

We are told that the ascetic yet cheerful life of these lovable, ardent, unworldly apostles of Jesus, who tramped the moors all day in order to preach to people in the evening, won the hearts of the men of the north. I am sure this was also true elsewhere. Indeed, it was said that Christianity had never, since its earliest years, appeared in a more attractive guise.

All this was undoubtedly a work of the Spirit. But it has always been true, all down the history of the Christian church from the Day of Pentecost, that wherever a genuine work of the Spirit breaks out, there are always those who want to bring it under control.

And so it proved to be in this case. The success of the Iona and Lindisfarne missions on English soil revived the dispute between the Celtic and Roman churches. So long as the Celtic church had remained in Celtic territory – beyond the border of Scotland – Rome could afford to overlook its remote existence. But when it broke out down south, and spread to the east and south-east coasts of England, in Rome's eyes a rivalry for the possession of Saxon England had begun.

Saxon England was Rome's preserve! Whatever happened, this independent Celtic church must submit to Rome. The issue could no longer be evaded. So once again the two streams of the Christian faith met in England and a struggle for supremacy began all over again. The tragedy was that all this was coming to a head at the very time when Anglo-Saxon England had turned away from the worship of Thor and Woden and had definitely rallied to the Christian faith. Indeed, this was the time of which it has been said: 'There was now no kingdom in which heathen practices prevailed. The whole Island was now Christian.'

The issue was no longer whether the island should be Christian or pagan, but whether the Roman or Celtic view of Christianity should prevail; whether British Christianity should conform with, and submit to, the Roman form of Christianity – which, by now, under the Bishop of Rome, dominated Christendom – or whether it should remain independent and free, and continue to be expressed through the type of Christianity on which the Celtic churches of the north had been founded.

To settle the matter, Oswy, King of Northumbria and brother of Oswald (now deceased), summoned the Synod of Whitby in 663. It hung for a long time in the balance but, in the end, King Oswy, who had championed the Celtic church of Iona since his brother's death, was tragically influenced by his wife, and gave his judgment that the church of Northumbria should be a definite part of the church of Rome and of the Catholic system.

This decision started a landslide. The church of Mercia conformed with it soon afterwards. Some of the outstanding Celtic Christians from Iona, like St Cuthbert, accepted the new order of things. The leader of the Celtic church and the remainder of his followers returned to Iona in disgust. When these Christians of Iona saw that their Northumbrian friends had so tragically turned against them, they realised they could no longer maintain the struggle for their particular stream of Christianity in England, and so they withdrew.

The synod's decision therefore meant that by far the greater and more powerful part of the island was now to be associated with the papacy. A major step had been taken towards this country becoming Roman Catholic, and in the course of succeeding generations Scotland, Wales and Ireland gradually came into line with the rest of Roman Catholic Western Europe. And this is the state of things which we find just prior to the Reformation. It is only fair to say, however, that the Irish clergy had originally refused to submit.

Trevelyan saw some of the far-reaching results of all this when he remarked: 'It cannot be denied that the decision of Whitby contained the seeds of all the trouble with Rome down the ages to come.' But there were consequences which were even worse than that.

Seeds sometimes have a habit of growing until they develop into great trees whose branches reach out so that they cover the whole land – indeed, many lands. To bring under control a work of the Holy Spirit is to quench the Spirit. To quench the Spirit – especially over a long period of time – is to extinguish the light, and extinguishing the light inevitably leads to darkness – sometimes to *great* darkness. Which is exactly what happened in this case.

Even before the early Tudor period in England had dawned, the original, pure, New Testament and biblical form of Christianity had become so overlaid with non-biblical and erroneous doctrine, and often with extra teachings, requirements and practices introduced by the popes and the Roman Catholic Church, that it became entirely obliterated and lost. In consequence, a period of great spiritual and moral darkness followed, not only in

Britain but also all over the continent of Europe, and wherever the Roman Catholic Church held sway. So by the time the Tudor period arrived, Britain had almost entirely lost her original – and essentially *biblical* – Christian foundations. Furthermore, she was a nation without a Bible in her own native tongue.

To understand that, is to understand what the Reformation was all about.

* * * *

God will not allow the light of his truth to be covered up and buried indefinitely. He always has a way of deliverance, and perhaps this is no more clearly demonstrated than in the English Reformation.

Far from being merely a political movement, as some may have been led to suppose, the Reformation was very much a spiritual revolution. It was, in fact, a revolution brought about by the Holy Spirit of God. When revealed in its true light, it can be seen as God moving to release his truth and to restore it as the only true foundation upon which people should build.

Darkness had closed in upon the land. But then the Spirit of God began to move upon the heart of a man, and this time, of a man on the Continent. The God who, at the time of creation, had caused the light to shine out of darkness, now shined in this man's heart. Martin Luther's eyes were suddenly opened to the glorious truth that rather than a man having to earn his salvation by his own personal efforts and merit, as Rome had taught, God's plan was that he could be saved eternally from the guilt, power, and eternal consequences of his sin by simply trusting in what the Lord Jesus Christ had done on the cross to atone for his sin. Luther suddenly saw that it was in *this* way that a man was made righteous in the sight of God, and could then be accepted by him.

When this brilliant light dawned upon Luther's soul, he believed it. He put his entire trust in it and the result was a new creation; he became 'a new creature' in Christ Jesus

(2 Corinthians 5:17). The scales had been removed from his eyes; old things had passed away, all things suddenly became new. His whole life and outlook were completely transformed and changed and he became filled with the Holy Spirit of God. In that way, there was a divine seal placed upon Luther that he was now God's son, and he knew it. He also knew that he had a mighty deliverance from bondage, and that he was now truly born again. This was, indeed, a revolutionary spiritual experience.

It was this experience of the new birth, in Luther's conversion, which sparked off that movement of the Spirit of God on the Continent which we now call the Reformation. The movement spread from Wittenberg to Geneva, began to take root in Scotland, and then came to England. In fact, historians record that the movement which Luther started was so dynamic, and spread so rapidly, that within the space of a mere ten years it had overrun the Continent. Right at its heart, all the time, was this basic *biblical* Christian teaching which had led to Luther's coversion – the doctrine of justification by faith in Jesus Christ, and only in Jesus Christ.

'It is *by faith*; it is *by faith*!', went up the cry. 'The just shall live by faith.' Luther had seen it, and it had revolutionised his life.

The rediscovery of this doctrine led to others, everywhere, entering into the self-same experience of the new birth. Very soon, thousands were being brought out 'from darkness to light, and from the power of Satan unto God' (Acts 26:18). Those who realised that they were estranged from God, found that they, too, could be reconciled and put right with him, simply by trusting in Jesus Christ in the same way that Luther had done and – as they later discovered – as the New Testament taught.

So countless lives were being miraculously changed and transformed, and that had a remarkable effect upon the Christian church. For the life of the church began to vibrate once again, first on the Continent, and then in *this* country. People everywhere were receiving this new life from God.

Furthermore, Luther's rediscovery of the vital doctrine of justification by faith led him to examine the whole question of authority in the church. For hundreds of years now, it was what the *church* said, that mattered. People must believe this and that because the church said so. They must always be guided by 'mother church', and the final court of appeal for settling matters in dispute was the pope.

Luther had received his revelation from the Bible. The Holy Spirit had lit up that vital verse: 'The just shall live *by faith'*, and he had believed it and was saved. He now saw that the *Bible* was the authority. So from now on the words of Scripture, not papal authority or the authority of the church, became his guiding light. When Luther made this truth known abroad, it sparked off a chain-reaction.

In the universities, the scholars of the day gave themselves to a re-examination of the Scriptures. This happened both on the Continent and here at home, leading to the Scriptures being translated from Latin into the common language of the day and being made available to the masses of the people so that, as we shall see, there was a great turning to the Bible amongst ordinary folk.

That is what the Reformation was all about.

It is well known that in 1517 Martin Luther denounced the Roman Catholic sale of Indulgences by nailing his thesis on this and other highly questionable matters to the door of Wittenberg Castle church. He began, therefore, by protesting against church practices, but his movement soon became a challenge to church doctrine – that is, to doctrine as it was being taught by Rome.

'Salvation by faith, not by works' was Luther's great theme. For the Bible says: 'A man is not justified by the works of the law . . . for by the works of the law shall no flesh be justified' – cleared of all sin in the sight of God – but it is 'by the faith of Jesus Christ' that he can be so cleared (Galatians 2:16).

The Lutheran doctrines had no sooner been proclaimed in Wittenberg, than they became a power in England. Although it is true that the Reformation *started* in this country with political issues, even those aspects proved to be of God. If we look a little more closely, we shall see why this was so. There had been a spirit of English nationalism abroad ever since Plantagenet times (from 1154 onwards) and it was now maturing. Men had been asking what British people are asking all over again today: 'Why should we look abroad for any part of our laws? Why not act through our own Parliament?'

In Henry VIII's day, the average Englishman retained the feeling of his Welsh and Celtic Christian ancestors against the pope's interference in England. So when Henry's divorce issue was at its height and was being strongly resisted by the pope, Henry himself, in his indignation, came to understand what many Englishmen had realised long before; that England, if she would be a nation indeed, must protect both spiritual and temporal jurisdiction from outside manipulation. As is so often the case in national affairs, it took a personal issue for Henry to see this so clearly.

Henry now found it intolerable that the interests of England should be subjected to the will of an outside power. The decisive moment had been reached. He made up his mind that England would no longer submit to being governed by a religious authority, or any other authority sitting hundreds of miles away, which judged English matters by Italian, Spanish, or French standards and interests, but never by English. To which we might well add the standards of Brussels and Moscow. These are the issues which have to be decided by this country today.

Henry therefore took measured steps until England was wholly independent of every kind of administration from Rome. When a Bill was finally passed through Parliament abolishing what still remained of papal authority in England, followed just a month later by a letter written personally by the king in which he described his position as 'King and Sovereign, recognising no superior in earth, but only God, and not subject to the laws of any earthly creature', the break between England and Rome was complete.

The way God used these political moves now becomes clear. At this stage the great revolution, called the English Reformation, freed the English church and state from the bonds of Rome, and ushered in the acceptance by England of the *Protestant* Christian religion. Christianity was now free to develop as it always should have been free to develop from the time of the Synod of Whitby, and the Reformation brought about a profound change. At the very time when the spiritual and moral darkness in England was most intense, God once again raised up a man. This time it was William Tyndale. Seeing the darkness with which his beloved country had become surrounded, Tyndale became gripped with the burning conviction that the entrance of God's Word into a man's heart brings light.

For centuries, the Scriptures had been denied to everyone but the priests, and even then they were in Latin. John Wycliffe, 'the Morning Star of the Reformation', and his Lollards had been instrumental in undertaking the work of translating the Bible into English earlier on. Now Tyndale was determined to see that the Bible was translated from the Latin into the Tudor English language of that day, in order that everybody should be able to understand it and that a copy should be placed in the hands of every man, woman and child in England. His desire was that even the poorest ploughboy should be able to read it.

He was hounded, harassed, and persecuted as he strove to get the work of translation and printing done, and was later driven to the Continent. There he resolutely and persistently continued his work and began shipping copies to England. It cost him his life, but just before he suffered martyrdom for his endeavours, he uttered this heart-rending prayer: 'O God: Open the King of England's eyes.'

God did not allow his servant's efforts to be thwarted; he answered his prayer. Within a year – at King Henry VIII's command – a copy of the Bible, translated into the language which everybody could read and understand, was chained to the lectern of every church in the land, and the king, backed by his government, enjoined the clergy to encourage Bible reading. Six copies of the Bible were set up in St Paul's Cathedral in the City of London, and multitudes thronged to the cathedral all day to read them, such was the hunger for the Word of God. Furthermore, when these people could find anybody with an audible voice to read aloud, their enthusiasm knew no bounds.

Tyndale, therefore, was used of God to fan the flame which Luther had already set alight. He was the first to give the Bible to England in Tudor English, and his heart-rending prayer is inscribed for all to see on a metal plaque in front of his statue in London's Thames Embankment Gardens.

Britain's foundations were being relaid. By 1535 the demand for complete printed Bibles was so great that copies of Tyndale's translation, and the one made by Coverdale, were running through several editions.

Under Henry, the Reformation continued apace in other directions as well. Having become (in the temporal sense) supreme head of the church, the heavy hand of his royal authority put away relic-worship, image-worship, paying sums of money for pardon to the priests, religious superstitions and such like. All over the country relics were destroyed, and 'miracle-working' images taken down. The cry went up: 'Dagon is everywhere fallen. Bel of Babylon is broken in pieces.'

The king also ordered fathers everywhere to teach their children the Lord's Prayer, the Ten Commandments, and the Articles of the Christian faith in English, *in their own homes*. Would that we could see this being done all over again today! And who says these things cannot be achieved by legislation?

But there was preaching involved in the Reformation as well. For we read that 'Hugh Latimer, preaching at St Paul's Cross to the citizens, and in the King's garden to the courtiers, by his rough, homely sermons, set the standard of that English pulpit oratory which, together with the Bible and the Prayer Book, effected the conversion of the people to Protestantism in the course of the next hundred years.'

It was the Bible, above all, which led to this profound spiritual and moral change in the nation. Historians say: 'We must credit the reign of Henry VIII with giving the English Bible to the people.' Trevelyan, in particular, comments: 'We talk much about Shakespeare and Shakespearian English, but our own historians proclaim that though Shakespeare may be in retrospect the greatest glory of his age, he was not in his own day its greatest influence. By the end of Elizabeth's reign, the Book of books for Englishmen was already the Bible.

'For every Englishman who had read Sidney or Spenser, or had seen Shakespeare acted at the Globe Theatre, there were hundreds who had read or heard the Bible with close attention as the Word of God. The effect of the continual domestic study of the Book upon the national character, imagination or intelligence for nearly three centuries to come, was greater than any literary movement in our annals, or any religious movement since the coming of St Augustine.'

As to the Bible's effect on people's language and thinking, Trevelyan goes on to say: 'New worlds of history and poetry were opened up in its pages to a people that had little else to read. Indeed it created the habit of reading and reflection in whole classes of the community, and turned a tinker into one of the greatest masters of the

English tongue.

'Through the Bible, the deeds and thoughts of men who had lived thousands of years before in the eastern Mediterranean, translated into English during the period when our language reached its brief perfection, coloured the daily thought and speech of Britons to the same degree as they are coloured in our own day by the commonplaces of the newspaper press.'

But with far more enobling effect, I might add!

So much did the Bible become part and parcel of the individual's life and character, that our literature became steeped in it, personal letters were full of quotations from it, and parliamentary speeches, until less than half a century ago, were punctuated and interwoven with it. The Bible became the very warp and woof of what we, as a nation, said and wrote down. For the sake of those who argue that we never have been a Christian country, let me quote Trevelyan once again in order to show that the Reformation period in England was a time when we came very near to it. He says: 'The conversion of England to Protestantism, which can be traced to origins in the time of Wycliffe, was substantially effected during the long reign of Elizabeth. When she died, *the majority* of the English regarded themselves as ardent Protestants, and *a great number of them* were living religious lives *based on the Bible and Prayer Book.*' (my italics) That speaks for itself.

It should have become quite clear by now, that what we are talking about is the restoration of our original, biblical, Christian foundations. God was undergirding the nation with them all over again. Or to put it another way, God was delivering us from that great period of darkness into which union with Rome, from Whitby onwards, had plunged us, and restoring to us that first stream of Christianity which had begun to flow in Britain at the time of Columba, and which may well have first been deposited here very soon after Pentecost and before the Roman occupation of Britain. That was original New Testament and biblical Christianity.

God even used the time when the printing press – not on this occasion the Roman roads – could aid it forward, and the time when the English language reached its perfection of force and beauty in the mouths of men, in order that this rediscovered, dynamic, New Testament message might be fully expressed.

It was our return to that original stream of Christianity – and our constant desire and determination to ensure that once fully restored, it should so remain – which resulted in our being called 'Protestant'. For Protestantism, in essence, means to take a stand for original biblical Christianity in its purest form, against all other forms which in any way deviate from it.

This is why our country became known, the world over, as a Protestant Christian country. And it is why we were so much hated by King Phillip II of Spain, who, during the reign of Elizabeth I, was the pope's military arm.

The Reformation in England meant that another important landmark had been reached in the history of our island, and in the history of Christianity in Britain. Under Queen Elizabeth I, England became, for the first time, a Protestant Christian country *by law*. That position has been zealously guarded, against all kinds of intrigue, throughout the succeeding centuries, and will, no doubt, need to be so guarded again.

As our British history clearly shows, God has intervened on more than one occasion to ensure that the Protestant Christian position should continue to be maintained. We shall see in Volume 2 that one of his interventions led to the defeat and rout of the Spanish Armada. I say we are a Protestant Christian country because God has made us so.

We should never forget, nor allow anyone else to forget, that our Protestant Christian position is still safeguarded today in that, by our British Constitution, the

Sovereign, and any successor, must be a Protestant.

Here I make bold to say that God may have to intervene yet again in order to keep it that way.

*   *   *   *

The Puritan period was also a time when this country's Christian foundations were being attacked and eroded. They were twice assailed by the royal house of Stuart, and, due to the strong forces working in the realm at that time, were in danger of being replaced by the erroneous teachings and practices of Rome. Yet God moved again, and right through this extremely turbulent period used such Christian luminaries as John Bunyan, Richard Baxter, John Milton, Thomas Goodwin, John Howe and John Owen to keep the true light of the Gospel burning. They, and many of the dissenting bodies, were the chief guardians of the truth at that time, and to remain faithful to it meant their being repeatedly dragged before judges' courts. For many of them it involved terms of imprisonment and being deprived of all their personal possessions. It also meant being forced out of their denominations, and particularly so, at the hand of Archbishop Laud, if they were members of the Church of England.

This period will be remembered, too, as the time when the opposition and persecution levelled against the groups of true believers who had separated themselves from the state church – such as the Baptists, the Presbyterians, and the Independents – were so fierce that many of their number were harried out of the land – some to Amsterdam, others to Leyden, and still more of them across the Atlantic in the *Mayflower* to New England. But there was a divine purpose even in this, for, as is well known, God used the Pilgrim Fathers to be the founders of the present United States of America, and to lay Christian foundations there.

Again, in the midst of all the turbulence at home, God

raised up that great Christian warrior, Oliver Cromwell. During his reign of office, popery and prelacy were prohibited, and Article XXXV of the Protector's Commonwealth Government declared that it was 'The Christian religion, as contained in the Scriptures, which was henceforth to be held forth as the public profession of the nation.' So once more, in an hour of extremity, God had taken steps to see that those original biblical foundations were made secure.

Chapter Six

The Great Awakening

The moral and spiritual tide in England immediately prior to the time of Wesley and Whitefield was at an extremely low ebb. In many ways, the condition of England was very similar to the condition in which we find it today. There are so many parallels, that when one reads the history of that period one gets the impression of reading a present-day account. The explanation is, of course, that history is repeating itself simply because fallen sinful men are still the same.

In the days preceding Wesley and Whitefield, as in the days of some of the Old Testament kings, the rot had set in right from the top. The first two Georges of the royal house of Hanover were unfaithful to their wives and had irregular attachments with other women. To use the blunt, unpolished description of the Bible, they were adulterers. Yet there was no outcry in the land. In fact, more than one historian has observed that one of the saddest comments on the condition of the country was that such disregard of moral sanctions in the royal house could be accepted by most people without question. Neither was there a John the Baptist to take these Sovereigns to task.

When corruption in a nation sets in at the top, it is soon reflected all the way down the line. So Thackeray said of

George II's moral laxity: 'No wonder that the clergy were corrupt and indifferent amidst this indifference and corruption. No wonder sceptics multiplied and morals degenerated.'

The rot had also started to affect the church, and basic Christian doctrines began to be discarded one by one. First, there was a departure from belief in the authority of Scripture. Men would rather build their beliefs on their own reasonings than on the authority of the Word of God. With this vital anchor cut, the nation was inevitably precipitated into an age of drift, and when other vital changes in Christian belief began to be made, these were regarded with comparative unconcern.

The nature and character of God began to be attacked. So-called Christian leaders and theologians began to deprive him of his essential attributes, making him to be a God after their own likeness and according to their own pathetic image.

The person of Jesus Christ came under attack. He was declared to be no more than a man, and therefore no longer to be regarded as God.

When once these three foundational Christian doctrines had been so seriously affected in the circles that mould Christian thought, the next thing that followed was that the supernatural and miraculous were almost entirely removed from Christian belief and outlook, with the result that essential New Testament faith was reduced to nothing more than humanism. Christianity, thus robbed of all that makes it dynamic and powerful, soon became a 'dead' religion. The salt had well and truly lost its savour, and Bishop Butler asserted that Christianity was wearing out of the minds of men. It was everywhere being held up to ridicule, and all that it stood for was being made the object of scorn. This, in turn, inevitably had its effect on the nation. Unbridled immorality, practised quite openly and unabashed, followed hard in the wake of a total disregard for God and of this widespread national ridicule and scepticism with regard to religion. Men glorified in their shame, and did so openly. Indeed, so openly defiant were they of decent moral laws and standards that they actually wanted to be known as loose and lawless. They boasted of being so. Had Jeremiah been with us at that time he would have asked: 'Were they ashamed when they had committed abomination? Nay, they were not at all ashamed, neither could they blush' (Jeremiah 6:15).

Stories abound of incredible vices and crimes being committed in the streets; robberies and brutal murders were being carried out wholesale. Violence was on every hand. The whole population seemed to be given over to one kind of orgy or another, and the very name of Englishman was made to stink in the nostrils of men of other nations.

All of this has a very familiar ring today. One can almost say: 'As then, so now.' In *both* centuries the various steps in our national decline are seen to be very much the same. Our literature, art, theatre, and almost all our culture, were so corrupt that they shocked even the most hardened of visitors from overseas. And against all this appalling evil the Christian church, as is also true today, was a totally powerless and ineffective weapon, either to fight against it or to stem the tide.

England, therefore, in the early days of the eighteenth century, had witnessed a decline in religion and public morality scarcely to be matched in the history of the nation. We had reached an all-time low. Such appalling corruption abounded that it seemed to call for nothing else but an outpouring of divine wrath. *We had become a nation ripe for judgment.*

Then, just at the point when things were at their worst, God began to move again in England. In 1735 the Spirit of God took hold of three men – George Whitefield, Howell Harris, and Daniel Rowland – in such a way that all were converted to Jesus Christ in that same year, although none of them knew this about the others at the time.

We shall see that God's purpose was to use all three, and others in their turn, for an itinerant ministry which was to bring about a great spiritual awakening in England, Scotland and Wales. This awakening is now referred to as the Eighteenth-Century Revival, and by the time that George III came to the throne in 1760, this great Evangelical Revival had swept the land.

So mercy had intervened instead of judgment.

The signs are that Britain is in a 'pre-eighteenth-century revival situation' today, and there are many who are praying for a similar revival. Indeed, Alexander Solzhenitsyn, the Russian author, Professor Arnold Toynbee, the historian, and the recent Archbishop of Canterbury, Dr Coggan, have each said that a revival of Christianity is the only hope for Britain and the western world. Solzhenitsyn has written: 'A moral and religious revival is the only salvation for the East, and also for the West.' But it must be a revival of true Christianity, and it must be brought about by the full power of the Holy Spirit. It may therefore encourage those who are praying and looking for such a revival today, to have a reminder of some of the extraordinary things that happened in the eighteenth century; to see what were some of its most outstanding features and far-reaching effects.

George Whitefield's dynamic new life began as the result of reading a book called *The Life of God in the Soul of Man*. Whilst reading it, he entered into an experience of the new birth and so became a man indwelt by the Holy Spirit of God. As a result of his being repeatedly 'endued with new power from on high', the impact which his life and preaching made on this country and on North America was tremendous.

People often refer to the awakening in England at that time as 'Wesley's Revival', but John Wesley was not then converted to God, neither was he to be for a further three years, and by that time the revival was well and truly under way. No, it was George Whitefield, and not John Wesley, who was used of God to *begin* the revival in

England. And for this reason Whitefield has gone down in history as 'the Great Awakener'.

Yet Whitefield had few indications of the remarkable way in which he was going to be used of God in England when, in 1736, a year after his conversion, he committed himself to go out across the Atlantic as a missionary to Georgia. In fact, just before his ordination as a deacon in the Church of England, he found he was not even able to compose a sermon!

All this was God at work. Like Ezekiel, he had the experience that 'Thou shalt be dumb, but when I speak unto thee, then thou shalt speak.' On the day of his ordination in Gloucester Cathedral he found he was still not able to preach; but the very next morning, some words from the New Testament came with great power to his soul: 'Speak out, Paul'!

Whitefield was not disobedient to this divine commandment. He preached the following Sunday to a crowded audience with as much freedom as if he had been a preacher for years. That sermon meant that the Great Awakening in England had now started, although Whitefield was not to know it at the time.

God then brought him to London although, to Whitefield, this move was only to make preparations for his forthcoming journey overseas. But God had other plans in mind for him and for this country before he could set out. In the providence of God, and due to unforeseen circumstances, Whitefield was to be kept in England for the whole of the following year.

Detained in London, Whitefield preached with great power in Bishopsgate Church and then in the Tower Chapel, which soon became crowded on Sundays as he continued there. So great was the response to his ministry in London that he stayed on for two months, preaching whenever and wherever he had an opportunity.

A new message was now shaking Britain, as it was yet to shake North America: 'You must be born again.' It was a message which was entirely fresh to the majority of people in Britain. They had never heard it before. At least that generation had not. It was entirely new to them because the true, dynamic Christianity of the New Testament which Britain had known in former days had become completely lost. So when people heard it being proclaimed again in the power of the Spirit, it literally startled them.

There was another element also. Each time Whitefield preached this 'new' message he was endued with great power from on high. That power came upon the crowds as they listened, and it brought about a mighty response.

Whitefield returned to his university – Oxford – and there the fire was kindled all over again in his heart.

From Oxford he went to Gloucester, merely, as he thought, to get his bishop's advice about going abroad. But God kept him in Gloucester for three weeks, preaching twice each Sunday, and we read that every time he preached, 'the power of God attended the Word.' There was this 'unction' which was given him from above, and the congregations in Gloucester became very large.

Whitefield went on to Bristol, but merely to take leave of some of his relatives before going overseas to North America. On reaching Bristol and attending a week-day service, as was his custom wherever he went, he was invited to come from his seat and preach.

The sermon startled his hearers. Next day he was invited to preach in another church, and many came to hear him. So great was the reaction to his sermon this time, that on the following Sunday many flocked from the other churches in Bristol to hear him.

All Bristol was now astir, and this widespread reaction to the 'new message' resulted in the mayor inviting Whitefield to preach in the presence of the Bristol Corporation. So Whitefield continued in Bristol for some time after this, preaching on week-days and twice on Sundays, mainly on the doctrines of new birth and of justification by faith in Jesus Christ alone. Again we read that during all this time 'the mighty power of God attended the Word.'

God now began to use the power of the printed word also, for the people in Bath and Bristol were so stirred by Whitefield's discourses that many asked if he would have his sermons printed, in order that they could both study them for themselves and also distribute them widely in the area. Thus was the fire spread still further.

Whitefield came to London again to make further preparations for going abroad, but God overruled again and circumstances kept him there for three weeks. He preached more frequently than before, and many came to hear him.

Soon he went down to Stonehouse in Gloucestershire, where so many came to listen that neither church nor house could contain the people, and each week the congregations increased. He said of this visit: 'I found uncommon manifestations of the power of God were granted me from above. Sometimes, like St Paul, it was as though I would be taken out of the body.'

Back at Bristol, he found a great hunger for the Word of God. The message seemed so new to them all that multitudes came on foot, with many more in coaches and on horseback. The congregations grew larger and larger. People of all ranks of society and of all denominations came flocking to hear his ministry. And the response was as great in Bath.

Whitefield was in London at the end of August 1737 to prepare to go overseas, but God intervened once more and his departure for America was still further delayed. He preached at St Ann's Cripplegate, Wapping, the Tower, Ludgate and Newgate, and all the time the congregations increased. By September even Fleet Street had begun to take notice and to mention his name in the newspapers. After three whole months of this continuous preaching, the crowds in the churches were so thick that

Whitefield felt he could almost walk on people's heads. In fact, London by now was so stirred that the streets were filled with people going to church long before daybreak. Copies of his printed sermons were being called for, and the awakening was spreading further and further afield. He was a new phenomenon in the Church of England. His message had literally startled the nation. All eyes were upon him.

By anointing his message on 'The Necessity of the New Birth,' and by anointing *him,* God was using Whitefield to restore England's original Christian foundations in the hearts of her people.

At this stage Whitefield had to go aboard the *Whitaker* for Georgia. But God had other plans, and other people, to ensure that the flames now kindled in the west country and in London did not go out while he took Whitefield to light a fire in America.

John Wesley landed in England the day before Whitefield sailed, but as a disillusioned man. He had spent more than two years as a colonial missionary in Georgia, but was now crying out in misery: 'I went to America to convert the Indians, but, Oh! who will convert me?'

Four months later came his spiritual birthday. On 24 May 1738, whilst he sat in an Aldersgate Street meeting-room listening to Luther's *Preface to the Epistle to the Romans* being read, he had a transfiguring experience. To quote his own words: 'At about a quarter before nine, while Luther in his Preface was describing the change which God works in the heart through faith in Christ, I felt my heart strangely warmed. I felt I did trust in Christ, Christ alone, for my salvation; and an assurance was given me that he had taken away my sins, even mine, and saved me from the law of sin and death. I began to pray with all my might . . . I then testified openly to all there, what I now first felt in my heart.'

Like Whitefield, he was born again of the Holy Spirit of

God, and was impregnated with spiritual fire that he, too, might be used to set England ablaze for God. He immediately began to preach that justification was by faith alone, and by so doing was used of God to fan the flames which Whitefield had already lit in 1737.

A second great wave of this mighty revival really began when Whitefield returned to England at the end of 1738. Having been used of God in America to begin a great spiritual awakening there, he returned, as he thought, only in order to be ordained priest at Oxford. But God had other plans.

He landed in Ireland from America in November, having survived a violent Atlantic storm, and his preaching in Limerick and Dublin caused a considerable stir. Arriving in London during December, he was greatly encouraged by the conditions which he found there. He soon perceived that, during his absence in America, God had watered the seed he had sown before his departure, and that as a result of the faithful ministries of John and Charles Wesley, many who had been converted under him a year ago had now grown to be strong men in Christ. A great outpouring of the Spirit followed his initial preaching at St Helen's Bishopsgate and Islington, and nothing short of a miraculous month followed. Despite the devil's activity in causing such resistance from the churches that all but four of them now excluded him from their pulpits, by the end of December Whitefield had preached in Spitalfields and across the river at Southwark, as well as at Bishopsgate and Islington, sometimes no less than nine times in one week, and with as great a power as ever he did in his life. The result was a constant stream of people coming to him for deep personal counselling between his preachings. So much was this the case that he had the firm conviction that it was only the prelude to something far bigger. There was a strong feeling within him that 'God was about to do great things amongst us.' He was not to be disappointed.

New Year's Day dawned. On 1 January 1739, at about three o'clock in the morning, there was a new outpouring of the Holy Spirit. Whilst some of them were in prayer at a 'love feast' being held in Fetter Lane, the power of God came mightily upon them. That outpouring of the Holy Spirit proved to be the precursor of the next wave of this heaven-sent revival. For a most remarkable year followed. One writer says, 'The new outpouring was a glorious preparation for the herculean work on which Whitefield and the Wesleys were about to enter.'

George Whitefield was indeed ordained priest at Oxford on 14 January 1739. In the afternoon he preached to a crowded congregation. 'God enabled me to preach with the demonstration of the Spirit and with power so that I could lift up my voice like a trumpet', he said. And while he preached, gownsmen of all degrees surrounded the church and stood at the windows attentive to every word.

He returned to London from Oxford and preached with great power to thronged congregations throughout the rest of January. At one church not only was the church itself packed, but there were nearly a thousand people in the churchyard. This led him to begin to think about preaching out of doors.

The crowning day of this part of his London ministry came, when on the first Sunday in February 1739, after preaching to vast congregations at Christ Church Spitalfields, St Margaret's Westminster, St Helen's Bishopsgate, and a full meeting-house in Fetter Lane, he wrote in his journal: 'God has owned me before nearly twelve thousand people this day.'

The opposition which arose amongst some church leaders and clergy against the doctrine of the new birth made clear what it was that was opening the eyes of so many people. For after Whitefield and Wesley had talked for a long time with their opponents, Whitefield said that the latter believed only in a Christ who was outside themselves, whereas 'we firmly believe He must be *inwardly* in our hearts.' This is a truth which needs to be rediscovered today.

It was just as this great climax was being reached in London that Whitefield prepared to set out towards the west country to go over the same ground he had covered previously. His arrival in Bristol during the second week in February 1739 was heralded by a letter which he received from one of his opponents. It read: 'Whitefield has set the Town on fire. Now he is gone to kindle a flame in the Country!'

It had been written in mockery, but it proved to be more prophetic than even Whitefield knew. His response to the letter was: 'I trust it is a holy fire that has proceeded from the Holy and Blessed Spirit. Oh that such a fire may not only be kindled, but blow up all England into a flame, and all the world over.' Certainly so far as England was concerned, he was to see his prayer wonderfully answered.

Opposition in Bristol, both from the Chancellor and the Dean of Bristol, caused Whitefield to be driven out into the open air. But in the providence of God this was in order that he might reach the colliers. To preach out in the open was the boldest step any preacher had taken at that time, but it proved to be the beginning of a great revival in the west country. First, two hundred colliers came to hear him at Kingswood; then between two thousand and five thousand people gathered; and within two weeks the crowds at Kingswood reached as many as ten thousand. Whitefield said: 'That man was right. The fire is kindled in the country, and I know all the devils in hell shall not be able to quench it.'

Going over to Hannan Mount and Rose Green Mount in his third week, the combined audiences amounted to no less than eighteen thousand in one day. After addressing fourteen thousand people at Rose Green Mount one Sunday afternoon he said, 'It was worthwhile to come so many miles to see such a sight. The more I am bidden to hold my peace, the more earnestly will I lift up my voice like a trumpet and tell the people what must be done in them, before they can be finally saved by Jesus Christ.'

God also overruled in the matter of his preaching in the Bristol churches, for despite the Chancellor's opposition, when he preached at St Mary Redcliffe it was like opening the sluice gates! Said Whitefield: 'I preached to such a congregation as my eyes never saw. Many went away for want of room.' He then preached to a great multitude inside St Philip's and St Jacob's church next day, but so many thronged to hear him that thousands had to go away because there was no room for them. All Bristol was by now astir.

Whilst this was going on, God was moving mightily in Wales. Howell Harris had been converted in the same year as Whitefield, and God was using him to re-lay the Christian foundations there. Whitefield now went to Wales because, he said, 'I want to catch some of Howell Harris's fire.' Crowds came wherever Whitefield went to preach, and he said he had never seen congregations so melted down. When leaving the Principality on 9 March his comment was: 'I think Wales is excellently well prepared for the Gospel of Christ. I bless God's Holy Name for sending me into this country.'

He went back to Bristol, and the awakening there continued apace. Over fifteen thousand colliers came to hear him preach on the first Sunday of his return; then during the next three weeks the numbers increased until, on Sunday 25 March, he preached in the open to over forty thousand people. The peak of his two months' ministry in that area came on his last Sunday, 1 April 1739, when, in all three places where he preached in the open, the congregations were larger than ever before.

It now became plain that God was bringing about an awakening in other parts of the kingdom. News had reached Whitefield of the wonderful progress which the Gospel was making in Yorkshire through the preaching of a man of God by the name of Ingham. He had seen what God was doing in Wales. Now news came to him of the way the Gospel was flourishing in Oxford. Later, he was told of how the Rev. Ebenezer Erskine had been driven out to preach in the fields in Scotland and had just spoken to fourteen thousand people! Christian foundations were therefore now being relaid everywhere. Whitefield now entrusted the work in Bristol to John Wesley, because the time for him to return to Georgia was fast approaching. He also persuaded Wesley of the necessity of field-preaching as the means most likely to reach the masses. Less than twenty-four hours after Whitefield had left Bristol, Wesley himself embarked on his own open-air preaching course, 'speaking from a little eminence in a ground adjoining the city to about three thousand souls.'

The text for this, the first of his many thousands of such field-sermons, was prophetic of the great things that lay ahead: 'The Spirit of the Lord is upon me, because he hath anointed me to preach the Gospel to the poor; he hath sent me to heal the broken-hearted; to preach deliverance to the captives, and recovering of sight to the blind; to set at liberty them that are bruised, to proclaim the acceptable year of the Lord.'

Whitefield visited Wales again and saw that the awakening there was now spreading everywhere. Then he spent the next fortnight blazing a trail back to London via Chepstow, Gloucester, Cheltenham, Oxford and their surrounding villages, thousands turning out to hear him wherever he stopped to preach. Arriving in London, he was once again driven by circumstances out into the open to preach. Then God worked most remarkably in London in just over a month.

On the first Sunday after his return, the numbers who came to hear him preach exceeded anything he had ever seen before. As many as twenty thousand came to Moorfields on the first Sunday morning, and there were never less than twenty thousand every Sunday morning throughout the whole of May. On Kennington Common there were at least thirty thousand people on that Sunday evening; by the next Sunday evening there were fifty thousand; and, a week later, sixty thousand. London was really being awakened.

At this stage, Whitefield was sometimes preaching for as long as an hour and a half or two hours, and multitudes of people would stand in the pouring rain, and even whilst it was snowing, in order to hear him. Rarely did anyone leave before he had finished. In fact, the people's hunger for spiritual things was so great that Whitefield said on one occasion: 'I felt they would listen all day to the Word of God being preached, if I could preach for that long.'

The climax to all of his London ministry came on the weekend beginning with the glorious first of June 1739. No less than eighty thousand people gathered at Mayfair near Hyde Park to hear him preach on that day, which was a Friday. Then on Sunday, 3 June he preached on Kennington Common to the largest audience he had ever seen in that place. No wonder he said at the end of this London visit: 'I have indeed seen the Kingdom of God come with power in this great city.'

And so Whitefield returned to Georgia. Hundreds, and perhaps thousands, had been converted under his ministry during the last half-year, and together with all that God was doing through Spirit-empowered preachers in other places, the whole of the British Isles was fast becoming ablaze for God.

Chapter Seven
A Changed Society

When Whitefield returned to America, Wesley took up the task and began traversing the land, mightily endued with the Holy Spirit of God. Up and down the country he went, riding on horseback, sometimes proclaiming salvation through Christ to savage Cornish smugglers, and at other times to drunkards and prostitutes in London. He preached to colliers at their pit-heads, to the down-and-outs in the Bristol slums. to the dockers and sailors of Liverpool, and to the 'wild, staring, blasphemers' of Newcastle upon Tyne. Soon this Gospel of salvation was being preached in every town and village in England; and everywhere Wesley's preaching, like Whitefield's, was being accompanied with great spiritual power. He constantly called for repentance and faith – repentance towards God and faith towards our Lord Jesus Christ – and numerous conversions followed.

Wesley was at home on horseback; disregarding rain and tempest, highwaymen and footpads, he journeyed unceasingly all over Britain. In all, he covered some 250,000 miles in the saddle, often over the most appalling of roads, and crossing no less than forty-two times to Ireland. He pursued this ministry for fifty years, and during his lifetime delivered some forty thousand sermons amongst people *where they were* – in the market places, on the commons, anywhere in the open where people would congregate. An ever-enlarging band of evangelists worked with him, and, as his converts mounted, he gathered them into groups – every group, when once it had grown spiritually strong, becoming a centre from which the new life in Christ spread to other lives. Thus through the simple testimony of common people to their new-found faith, longing souls were set alight everywhere. And all the time it was the pungent doctrines of uncompromising biblical Christianity which Wesley, like Whitefield, was consistently setting forth. He was therefore continuing methodically to re-lay Britain's Christian foundations. In fact, Sir C. G. Robertson, in his *Oxford History of England*, has written: 'At a time when Bishop Butler asserted that Christianity was wearing out of the minds of men, Wesley kept the English people Christian.'

Eventually it was not just Wesley who was doing it. Wesley had a vision, and the vision was that every convert should become a soul-winner; every Christian should be a crusader for Christ. This vision was based on the New Testament teaching of 'the priesthood of all believers', and Wesley so put the teaching and the vision into operation that eventually he had an army of no less than 8,600 bringing the impact of the Gospel to bear upon the people of this country. That was one of the secrets of the revival's great spiritual depth, and of why it spread so quickly.

We need to remember that Wesley's Christianity was a Bible-based Christianity. Wherever the revival spread, its first avowed aim was to dispel the appalling spiritual ignorance which was abroad, by an ever-increasing knowledge of the Bible. A Bible religion demanded a thorough knowledge of the Scriptures. Wesley himself taught that one could never be a 'thorough Christian' without extensive reading. This conception set thousands of converts to the task of teaching themselves to read, so that they might search the Scriptures and other books which were designed to strengthen their moral and spiritual lives.

The Bible therefore became central to countless

people's lives. To the individual Christian it was the hand-book of moral and spiritual guidance, and because it was, his personal Bible became very much underlined. To the family and the Christian household, the Bible was the medium of family worship. To evangelical Christian society as a whole, the Bible was regarded as both chart and compass in the journey through life.

Wesley and Whitefield's ministry, therefore, together with that of other Spirit-filled preachers, ushered in a period of great spiritual revival and strength, the like of which had never been experienced in this country before. Historians speak of it as 'the great work of grace which transformed England in one of the darkest periods of its history.'

It was a time when 'evangelical Christianity, that is, Bible-based Christianity, laid hold upon multitudes of Englishmen with a firmer grasp and in a greater number of instances than ever before.' With regard to its far-reaching effects, one assessor of this period has said: 'The fires of the Revival had been kindled from heaven, and before the accession of George III the churches had caught the flame. Their ministers were beginning to preach with a new fervour, and their preaching was followed by a new success. The religious life of the people was becoming more intense. A passion for evangelistic work had taken possession of church after church, and by the end of the century the old meeting houses of non-conformity were crowded; many of them had to be en-larged, and new meeting houses had to be erected in town after town, and in village after village, in every part of the country.'

So great, in fact, was the permeating influence of this Evangelical Revival, that Nonconformity, with its primary emphasis on the New Testament and on the Spirit of the Gospel, became again a power in the land and a force to be reckoned with at the very highest levels.

This mighty baptism of fire also revived spiritual vision,

and kindled a great Christian initiative among thousands in the national church; but what is even more important, it reclaimed, for God, multitudes outside the churches who had long been beyond the pale of any immediate spiritual influence. So countless numbers both outside and inside the churches were ultimately affected by the Awakening. Indeed, the revival finally transformed the whole tone of the national life of the country. All areas and departments of life were cleansed, which, as we have seen from the earlier description of England's appalling decline and condition, was the country's direst need. And this is, of course, the most urgent need of our country today.

But it is necessary, in view of a great deal of wrong thinking today, to maintain a clear understanding of exactly how this great national transformation of Wesley's day came about. For Wesley and Whitefield did not believe, as do some in high ecclesiastical and governmental positions today, that it is a man's environment, surroundings and social circumstances which largely determine his character and the way he behaves. Rather they saw that it was the other way about, because they knew that the teaching of the Bible and their own experience of the new birth clearly showed that this was the case. It was not a question of changing society in order to change the behaviour and character of men, but rather a matter of changing *men*, and then *they* would do something about changing their society. Both Whitefield and Wesley saw what the Lord Jesus Christ had clearly taught before them, that the real problem was the human heart. It is out of the heart of a man, out of his innermost being, said Jesus, that all evil things proceed. All these evil things come from within. So the eighteenth-century revival centred Christianity in the individual human heart, not in the state or the environment, and not even in the church. And we need to capture this vision – this basic principle of the Great Revival – again today.

To go even deeper, Wesley and Whitefield saw clearly that men's hearts, because of inbred sin, were estranged and cut off from God; so both of them constantly sought, first and foremost, through the preaching of the cross of Jesus Christ in the power of the Holy Spirit and through its message of atonement, to bring individual souls into an abiding, personal communion with God. This is why their emphasis all the time was on *preaching*. And that is where it needs to be today.

They knew that the central promise of God in the glorious news concerning the new covenant was 'A new heart will I give you, and a new spirit will I put within you', and they knew that for the individual who believed, it was preaching that would bring that promise about. God's method as laid down in the New Testament had always been: 'It pleased God by the foolishness of preaching to save them that believe' (1 Corinthians 1:21), and they realised that this was still God's method.

Their chief and constant concern, therefore, as they preached, was to see the hearts of men changed as a result of individual conversions. For both saw clearly that a man must have the Spirit of the Lord Jesus Christ dwelling within him before he can ever call himself a Christian. They saw that true Christianity was literally the life of God himself being implanted within the innermost soul of a man, and then developing until it brought forth fruit in terms of a new life and Christ-like character. After all, it was seeing this which had led to Whitefield's conversion. Or to put it another way, they saw that the *real* Christian life was the Lord Jesus Christ living out his life from within the heart of a Christian. It was that which made the Christian's life dynamic, and it was that which made it entirely new. And Wesley and Whitefield knew that this new life could only begin with the new birth – with conversion – for they understood that *that* was when the individual, as he believed the message preached, became a partaker of the divine nature (2 Peter 1:4).

Personal conversion, therefore, not social revolution, was Whitefield's and Wesley's primary aim.

As to changes in society, it must be realised that England, before Whitefield's awakening commenced, was almost totally bankrupt of strong moral and spiritual convictions, in much the same way as she is today. Therefore these vital convictions had to be created first, before any of the desperately needed changes and transformations in society could be brought about, or before England could hope to see any turning of the spiritual and moral tide.

Wesley, as much as anybody else, was deeply concerned about the evils and injustices which surrounded him in his day; perhaps even more so, if the truth were known. But he saw clearly that when once men had been brought to the experience of personal conversion to Jesus Christ in sufficient numbers, and, as a result of that conversion, had had their consciences awakened to all the evils and social injustices which were around them, they would automatically and spontaneously begin to do something about changing the evils. 'Give me a hundred men who fear nothing but God and Hell', he said, 'and we will change the world.' So he devoted himself whole-heartedly to travelling his 250,000 miles, preaching his forty thousand sermons in the open, amongst people where they were. Praise God for the changed lives that resulted. The strong moral and spiritual convictions of which England had become so bankrupt were created all over again! Multitudes of people came to a new faith in Jesus Christ, and that new faith gradually created a new conscience as, in all parts of the country, the revival of Christianity changed hearts and gave a new sense of direction and purpose to the lives of great numbers of people. There arose an abiding concern for righteousness within countless souls throughout the land, as newly awakened consciences became more and more aware of the moral evil and social sin which was all around them, and at the same time an overwhelming desire and determination to put things right. And that is what led to change.

That is the order in which things happened then, and that is the order in which, if God gives us the time, we need to see that they happen all over again today.

How did this work out in detail? As is commonly known, a whole series of reforms was ushered in. But it should never be forgotten that these reforms were brought about by changed men. It was through changed men that the abolition of the slave trade came about. William Wilberforce, Zachary Macaulay, Henry Thornton, John Venn, and the other leading champions who fought for the abolition of the British slave trade, were all products of the eighteenth-century revival. Each one in turn had been born again of the Holy Spirit of God under the Spirit-filled preaching of the revival, and it was from a personal Christian faith that all derived their initial inspiration and drive for this courageous venture.

It was through changed men and women that our British prison system became more humanised, and that our British penal code became drastically reformed. The revival of true Christianity had led men to see the spiritual value which man must put on his fellow-man. More than any other religious movement which the English-speaking world has yet known, the Great Awakening emphasised the equal and priceless value in the sight of God of every person, and that the individual is responsible to God for the way his fellow-man is treated. England, at the time of the Awakening, had a particularly ferocious and cruel criminal code. Wilberforce repeatedly joined others in inveighing against it, and thorough-going evangelical Christians worked steadfastly with the robust humanitarian radicals of the day to remove the inhuman and grossly unjust features of our vicious and tyrannical penal system.

John Howard, the champion of prison reform and another evangelical Christian, was a zealous disciple of

John Wesley and a Spirit-filled man. He too was gripped with this burning desire to see that his fellow-men were being properly treated. That is why he travelled thousands of miles to inspect the jails of the entire United Kingdom, and that is why he expended much of his personal fortune in furthering the prisoner's cause and in bringing about reforms.

That is why Elizabeth Fry followed closely in John Howard's wake, spending a great deal of her time reading the Bible to some of the most depraved human beings in prison, and praying with them. She caused true Christianity to have a miraculous effect on the most degraded of prisoners, and particularly in London's Newgate Prison. It was this Christ-like compassion and personal concern for the well-being of others, and particularly for those in distress and who were living in appalling conditions, which inspired the Christian movement towards reforming our prisons and penal code.

It was through changed men that great advances began to be made in the realm of education. Before God sent the great revival, the moral and spiritual decline which was in progress at that time had inevitably caused education to reach an extremely low ebb. Multitudes of adults, let alone children, could not even read. When revival came, and the spiritual awakening spread, there arose – as we have seen – a great longing to read the Bible. This longing generated a persistent craving for popular instruction and teaching, and that craving Wesley was determined to satisfy. He set thousands of his adult converts the task of teaching themselves to read, and made ceaseless use of the printing press in order to supply them with good Christian literature. Tens of thousands must have taught themselves to read from these various publications. Every home which had been deeply affected by the revival had its little collection of much read books, and some of these collections are still in existence today.

Wherever Wesley's teaching penetrated, parents first

desired that their own children should be educated; then they had a similar desire for education to be given to the neglected youngsters around them. The result was a steady increase in schools.

Popular education in England, therefore, grew directly out of the Evangelical Revival itself, and was pioneered by the revival's practical, vital, New Testament Christianity. On all sides, this rebirth of real, dynamic Christianity advanced the efforts for education which Wesley encouraged. The establishment of the Sunday schools movement is an example of this.

This movement first taught reading and writing as well as a knowledge of the Bible; and in the process it grew amazingly. Wesley reported in 1784 that he found these schools springing up everywhere he went, and he lived to visit and examine local Sunday schools with nearly a thousand children in attendance, and with about one tenth of that number of voluntary teachers. George III, a promoter of the revival, gave the movement a further impetus when, in 1805, he made his famous statement: 'It is my wish that every poor child in my dominion shall be taught to read the Bible.'

The movement continued to grow until it became first national and then international; all as a direct product of the revival. When children employed in the factories were eventually set free from child-labour by Lord Shaftesbury's Factory Act in 1847, one of the principles central to that particular piece of reform was 'that children should be freed, and educated nobly to take their place as intelligent, useful, healthy and happy citizens in a Christian State.' Voluntary schools had by this time already come into existence. When the Board School Acts of 1870 were passed, they had as their purpose 'to complete the voluntary system and to fill up the gaps, but not [present parliamentarians and ministers of education please note] to supplant the voluntary system.' Britain therefore owes it to the eighteenth-century revival of Christianity that she ever had a system of popular education.

Then it is to changed men that Britain owes, or owed, its voluntary hospital system. Sir George Newman observed that 'an unprecedented improvement in public health accompanied the progress of the Eighteenth-Century Revival', and it was due to the effect of this revival upon it that 'the splendid, voluntary hospital facilities of modern England came to be more associated with a spiritual rather than with a materialistic concept of life.' And J. W. Bready says: 'The British voluntary hospital system – the only major hospital system in the world which was supported almost exclusively by the free will gifts of an appreciative public – was a product of the Evangelical Revival.'

It was John Wesley who started the first free medical dispensary in England. It was he who established the first centres offering free electrical treatment to the poor. He it was who constantly emphasised the sanctity of the human body as the temple of the living Spirit of God, urging the Christian duty of keeping it healthy and pure.

All these things therefore were introduced into the land by a changed man, and were afterwards developed and expanded by changed men.

Then it was through changed men that we got our modern voluntary social services organisations, welfare systems and facilities. For, as J. W. Bready writes, 'The voluntary hospital system, which is the best known of the voluntary-humanitarian services of Britain, is but symbolic of a unique heritage of modern social service organisations, in the creation of which, nineteenth-century England led the world.'

The same Christian awakening which had inspired and led the abolition of the slave trade, which had humanised the prison system and brought about penal reform and which had laid the foundations of popular education, had also inspired the many modern philanthropic and social service movements of which Dr Barnado's Homes, the

Shaftesbury Society, the National Society for the Prevention of Cruelty to Children, the Salvation Army, and the London City Mission are but a few. All these were brought into being by people who were possessed by the compassionate Spirit of Jesus Christ and who were filled with revival fire. All of them seek to go to the rescue of, or bring relief to, others.

Let it not be forgotten in this modern age of industrial strife, that it was also changed men who, at that time, brought vast improvements to the country's entire industrial system and who caused England's 'industrial slaves' to be set free. The long struggle for the emancipation of the factory workers from unjust and intolerable working conditions was essentially a Christian programme in character, and its Christian standpoint was made the cardinal emphasis throughout.

The crusade was led by Lord Shaftesbury, a thoroughgoing Christian who repeatedly described himself as an evangelical of evangelicals. He profoundly influenced the social welfare, not only of the British people, but of English-speaking peoples everywhere, and became known as 'the Great Emancipator'. But Shaftesbury became an emancipator of his fellow-men because he himself had first been set free by Jesus Christ and in consequence had become a changed man.

How many people today realise that the statue of Eros in London's Piccadilly Circus is a memorial to the monumental work of the great Shaftesbury and all that he did, as a Christian, to obtain the emancipation of his fellow-men from grim working conditions? The statue depicts an arrow of Christian love piercing the world, which is what Shaftesbury's love for his fellow-men sought to do.

Gladstone's tribute to Lord Shaftesbury is to be seen today inscribed round the base of this memorial: 'During a public life of half a century he devoted the influence of his station, the strong sympathies of his heart, and the great power of his mind, to honouring God by serving his fellow-men; an example to his order, a blessing to his people, and a name to be by them ever gratefully remembered.'

Shaftesbury was the inspiring, impelling, and sustaining force behind the Factory Act, the Mines and Colleries Act, the Chimney Sweep's Act, and a score of other important legislative enactments which his ceaseless endeavours on behalf of the working people of this country placed on the Statute Books of Britain.

He was a product of the Evangelical Revival, but so, too, were a good 90 per cent of the colleagues who worked with him in this heroic effort to free the 'industrial slaves'. So the tribute to Shaftesbury, put there in Piccadilly Circus by the freed factory operatives of Britain, stands also, in a very real sense, as an abiding testimony to the eighteenth-century evangelical revival.

We have said that it was changed men who changed conditions in the factories. Their entire campaign was conducted on Christian lines, without violence, either of speech or of action. And – let it please be noted – strikes, lock-outs, mob tactics, intimidation and threats were all regarded as 'out'. A deeply religious and Christian spirit permeated the humblest ranks of the crusade, and when a great national conference of factory operatives was held in London shortly after the passage of the 1847 Factory Act, a great note of thanksgiving to Almighty God was struck. This found its supreme expression in a resolution which was unanimously passed at that conference and which I quote in full because it seems to me that it needs to go on record again today: 'That we are deeply grateful to Almighty God for the success which has hitherto attended our efforts, and now that the object of our labours for the last thirty years is about to be brought to a happy consummation, we pledge ourselves to promote by every means in our power those religious and social blessings which it was the object of the Bill to extend to the factory worker.'

What further testimony is needed to the fact that it was

a Christian spirit which pervaded the whole of this crusade? In this age of industrial strife and unrest it cannot be emphasised enough that Shaftesbury and his colleagues freed the 'industrial slaves' entirely by constitutional and Christian means without a protracted strike, without a lock-out, without civil war, and certainly without the loss of a single life. All these ugly things were avoided, and it was because of this that there was left behind no legacy of resentment, and no smouldering hate after the Factory Act had been passed. Rather, there remained a firm foundation, largely of Christian principles, on which succeeding social attainments and changes could be built.

The 1847 Factory Act, and the comprehensive Ten-Hour Programme which was eventually embodied in it, went down in history as 'The Magna Carta of the Industrial Worker's Liberty', and we need to be reminded today of some of the things which it involved. It included the closing-down of factories between the hours of 6 p.m. and 6 a.m., and the keeping of them closed between these hours so as to put a stop to all night-work. It suppressed the guileful practice of 'shifts' and 'relays'. It guaranteed evening leisure; established practical immunity from Sunday labour; enforced a weekly day of rest; and won for British factory workers the Saturday half-holiday, thus providing a prolonged weekly period for recreation and sport long before any other country had even dreamed of such a benefit.

All these things were obtained for the worker by Christian men, and none of these things had been in operation before the Act was passed. In addition, the Act suppressed the very vicious practice of the 'free' use of women and children as 'fodder for industry'. And it is a point worthy of particular note by those who are deeply concerned about the breaking-up of family life today, that a principle central to Shaftesbury's radical crusade of social reform was 'that women should be freed from the tyranny of industry, and be educated to raise home-making to the standard of a Christian art or skill.'

The Factory Act also initiated the practice of compulsory education, both juvenile and adult, when once it had freed the children from child-labour. But soon after all this social and industrial legislation had been put through Parliament, chiefly under Lord Shaftesbury's leadership, a whole programme of other social welfare began to flow from it. Innumerable friendly and benefit societies, and a hundred self-help and co-operative movements began to come into being, as well as workers institutes, temperance guilds, literary and debating societies and, indeed, the sane, self-governing, British trade union movement.

The great lesson which the eighteenth-century awakening teaches us, therefore, is that the souls of men had had first to be awakened and created anew before this train of social reforms could be set in motion. Men were changed first, when the Christian Gospel was preached amongst them in the power of the Holy Spirit. Then changed men began to change their society. *That* is the order in which things happened.

How many people today appreciate that our British trade-unionism was a direct product of the Evangelical Revival, and that it has its very roots in Christianity? We have already drawn attention to the fact that, under the impact of Wesley's preaching, Nonconformist chapels all over the country grew and were multiplied. The British trade union movement grew directly out of these very chapels. No doubt there are some union members today who might find it convenient to forget these origins, but it is a fact which can neither be disputed nor denied. One of their leading members has given strong testimony to the fact.

Jack Lawson, a leading trade unionist who held office in the first Labour Government of 1924, traced trade-unionism's origins to the chapels in this way: 'The Evangelical Revival of the Eighteenth Century saturated the industrial masses with a passion for a better life – personal, mental, moral and social. The chapel was their first social centre, where they drew together, found strength in their weakness, and expressed to each other their hidden thoughts and needs. Here men first found the language and art to express their antagonism to grim conditions and injustices. The most powerful force for the mental and moral elevation of the workers during the industrial era has been the chapel' (contemptuously called 'Little Bethel', he said).

So it was in the chapel – in the house of God – that the trade union movement had its beginnings. What is more, the majority of the early leaders were Christians and, as such, were not only members of their local Free Churches but were also either preachers of the Gospel or were doing other active Christian work in their neighbourhood. They had Whitefield, Wesley, and other original founders of what was then the Christ-centred, deeply spiritual, Bible-based Methodist movement as their immediate spiritual ancestors. The entire trade union movement in this country is rooted and grounded in Christianity.

The great Lloyd George also testified to its *Christian* origins. Here is what he said: 'John Wesley inaugurated a movement that gripped the soul of England, that deepened its spiritual instincts, trained them, and uplifted them. That movement which improved the conditions of the working classes, in wages, in hours of labour, and otherwise, found most of its best officers and non-commissioned officers, in men trained in the Christian institutions which were the result of Wesley's Methodism.' Then he added: 'I never realise the effect which Methodism has had upon the national character so much as when I attended international congresses . . . and it is all due to the great religious revival of the eighteenth century.' By 'Methodism' he meant, of course, the dynamic New Testament Christianity which Wesley and his Methodist Societies revived and then applied at every level in the country.

The Christian origins and character of the trade union movement of England was nowhere made more dramatically conspicuous than when British unionists entered into international conference with the leaders of organised labour on the Continent. In 1910, for instance, 260 British trade union delegates visited the industrial city of Lille in the north of France. Like their continental comrades, the British deputation carried the socialist flag and many trade emblems. But when they appeared in the streets, the continental labour leaders were dumbfounded! For the British deputation also carried a banner which read: 'We represent 500,000 English workmen! We proclaim the Fatherhood of God and the Brotherhood of Man! Jesus Christ leads and inspires us.'

That Christian testimony really shook the continentals! To that extent were British trade union delegates determined to bring Jesus Christ to the fore. Moreover, in conference, some of the veteran British leaders, quoting freely from the Bible, declared stoutly that it was their Christianity which had made them trade unionists, cooperators, and socialists. That was in 1910, and British trade-unionism had arisen in England over 90 years before – in the years immediately following 1815. For so long, therefore, had trade-unionism's Christian origins and character been preserved. For almost 100 years, the impact which the Evangelical Revival made upon Britain's working community had an abiding effect.

So this great spiritual movement continued to cause the spirit and teaching of our Lord Jesus Christ to penetrate all departments of life. Having permeated the prisons, released the slaves, brought better working conditions into the factories, established hospitals and social welfare services, it spread the faith, vision and power of vital, dynamic, New Testament Christianity into the world of business and of economics, into the realm of politics, and into all national and even international affairs. In all these realms, and in many others, Christian foundations were well and truly laid, or re-laid.

The eighteenth-century revival can claim a whole series of 'firsts' to its credit. In the realm of politics, for instance, the first two men to represent British trade unionists in Parliament were Christians – Alexander Macdonald and Thomas Burt. They were returned after the general election of 1874. So it is correct to say that the first two Labour MPs ever to sit in the House of Commons were Christians; although they were called 'Lib-Labs' at that time, since no independent Labour Party then existed.

When the completely independent Labour Party was formed, the man who inspired and led the movement – Keir Hardie – was a Christian. He then became the first Independent Labour representative to sit in the House of Commons. This was in 1892, when he was elected MP for West Ham.

A year later, in 1893, Hardie became leader of the newly formed Labour Party in the House of Commons. So the first leader of the Labour Party was a Christian. And then Charles Fenwick, a Christian, was the first Labour MP to preside over a House of Commons committee.

Britain's first Labour prime minister, J. Ramsay MacDonald, and three times prime minister of England, was also a Christian. Referring to the effect which the Evangelical Revival had had upon the people of this country, Ramsay MacDonald wrote: 'That Common Baptism into one Free Faith, mediated by those intrepid modern apostles, Wesley and Whitefield, gave men self respect and pride. It did not merely arm them with claims for sharing in this world's goods. The problem . . . will never be solved by rectifying differences in status, or in material possessions. Class conflicts will only mislead us, and give victories which will be barren of results. The generation which loses the spirit of life loses everything worth having.'

These are words which many, surely, need to weigh again today.

But then he issued a warning which needs to be sounded out all over Britain in this so-called progressive age: 'Let us not pride ourselves that we are progressing if we let go the interests and inspiration which brought the Free Churches into being' – by which he meant the very spirit of the revival itself.

Referring to the Christian inspiration behind true democracy, he said: 'Democracy conquered the foothills . . Can it afford now to dispense with that ardour and devotion which only profound religious [Christian] belief and stern ethical principle can provide?' Such strident warnings need to be sounded out to a generation which, once again, has thrown away all its Christian foundations.

The first editor of Labour's daily newspaper, the *Daily Herald* – George Lansbury – was a Christian.

All these men, in one way or another, were products of the continuing baptism of fire which Whitefield and Wesley had originally been used to initiate; and they brought strong Christian influence to bear in other parts of society.

For instance, Alexander Macdonald was for a long time the leader and spokesman of miners all over Scotland. As such, he was elected president of the National Union of Miners, and remained so for eighteen years. As a Christian member of Parliament, he also represented the Scottish miners in Parliament for seven years.

Thomas Burt, that Bible-loving Christian, was for forty-eight years the secretary of the Northumberland Miners' Association. He later became president of the Trades Union Congress. So God was raising these Christian men into positions of leadership and influence in these spheres also.

Keir Hardie, a year after his conversion from atheism to Christianity, was elected secretary of the Ayrshire Miners' Association, so yet another Christian was giving leadership to the miners at that time. In fact, Jack Lawson, the trade unionist already quoted, speaking of the time when Christian socialists and evangelical trade union leaders were most vitally active, and of the time when the Christian influence in the trade union movement of Britain was at its strongest, said: 'The Gospel expressed in social terms has been more of a driving power in northern mining circles, than all the economic teaching put together.'

Such was the strong Christian leadership being given to the miners in those days, and to that extent was the mining industry being permeated by the Spirit of Jesus Christ. Let it please be noted that men like Alexander Macdonald and Thomas Burt loathed class-hatred and class-war. Neither of them would have tolerated the social reforms of the day being carried out along those lines – and most certainly Shaftesbury would not have done so – because to all these men, such class-hatred and class-warfare were foreign to the Spirit of Jesus which was in them.

We have already seen that Ramsay MacDonald was another Christian and product of the Evangelical Revival whom God raised up to a position of influence and leadership. As a young man, he was a pupil-teacher in his local kirk in Scotland, and it is beyond dispute that spiritual and moral forces had been uppermost in shaping all that was most attractive in his life. As a Labour MP, and later as Britain's first Labour prime minister, he found the materialism, economic determinism, class-hatred and atheism of Karl Marx's doctrinaire dogma to be quite repulsive, and was a strong advocate in Parliament for Christian ideals and principles. In fact, when he was prime minister he went so far as to say that he believed that democracy itself – true democracy – had its source in the eighteenth-century revival; that vital Christianity was indeed its very foundation; and that without Christianity, democracy is doomed to perish.

In a foreword to a book on George Whitefield, by Dr Belden, he wrote: 'The Free Churches were one of the pure sources from which free Democracy came. It was by the dynamic of free religion [by which he meant Christianity] that masses were inspired to escape from the quagmire of misery and injustice. The Christian Faith preserved the masses from becoming soul-less things obedient to the convenience and advantage of economic forces.'

That was by no means all from which the Christian faith preserved the masses in Britain. For history shows that when God intervened by sending revival to this country, he saved Britain from being engulfed in the kind of blood-bath that had overtaken France at the time of the French Revolution.

The impact which the Evangelical Revival had upon this country and upon its people, therefore, was incalculable. It was clear to all who were living at that time that there was a mighty power at work in the land, and it is no exaggeration to say that the effect which this great visitation of God made upon the country through the ministries of both Whitefield and Wesley lasted for well over 100 years.

Many testimonies have been written to the force of that impact. Writing of the revival's far-reaching effects, Trevelyan, in his *British History of the Nineteenth Century*, says: 'It was one of the turning points in the history of the world.' Then he said of Britain, after she had abolished the slave trade: 'Her command of the sea, her far-flung Empire, her mounting industrial power, her commercial supremacy, her inventive genius – *above all, her increasing moral stature, and her expanding spiritual vision* – won her a place of unique leadership amongst the nations. More than any other great nation in the middle of

the nineteenth century, she was worthy of world power.'
(my italics)

In other words, Britain was then in the ascendancy in
her position amongst the nations, and her rise to a position of world power can be traced directly to the time of
the Evangelical Revival. If she was worthy of world power
at that time, it was because God had raised her up into
that position. Many other such testimonies have been
written. But the greatest testimony I know, and the most
inspiring, is the one to be found engraved in marble for all
to see just inside the north doors of Westminster Abbey.
There on the huge memorial to William Pitt we can read
these words: 'During whose administration, and in the
reigns of George II and George III, Divine Providence
exalted Great Britain to an height of prosperity and glory
unknown to any former age.'

I say 'inspiring' because, let it be noted, this was precisely the period in our history which coincided exactly
with the Great Awakening which God granted us under
the preaching of Whitefield and Wesley. Let every
Englishman today dwell deeply on the words and implication of that inscription.

Let us also remember that as a direct result of this
revival of Christianity, England became a missionary-
hearted country, and so caused the impact of that revival
to be felt throughout the world. For whereas at the
beginning of the eighteenth century, and for a number of
years afterwards, there was not a single Protestant
missionary in the entire world (with the exception of a
small German group of the Moravian Brethren), by the
end of the eighteenth century the Baptist Missionary
Society, the London Missionary Society, the Scottish
Missionary Society, the Church Missionary Society and
the Religious Tract Society had all been founded within
the space of twelve years. From these sprang the whole
Protestant foreign missionary world movement, and from
these various societies, Britain began to send missionaries

to the far corners of the world. Thus, from this country, continent after continent began to be penetrated for Jesus Christ. The Evangelical Revival, therefore, did what neither the Reformation in the sixteenth century nor Puritanism in the seventeenth century did. It gave birth to a world-wide missionary zeal.

Moreover, as a result of this revival, the British people themselves became known the world over as 'the people of one Book, and that Book the Bible'; and it was directly due to the revival's influence that it was being said all over the world at that time that 'an Englishman's word is to be trusted; his word is his bond.'

All this had happened because God had mightily intervened in our history to ensure that the Christian foundations which had originally been laid, and which were again in danger of disappearing and of being entirely whittled away, were completely and gloriously restored.

As Queen Victoria put it in a message to two African chiefs: 'England has become great and happy by the knowledge of the true God and Jesus Christ.' Or perhaps she should rather have said: England has become great and happy because she has *rediscovered* the knowledge of the true God and Jesus Christ.

Chapter Eight
The Trumpet Sounds for Britain

Blow ye the trumpet in Zion, and sound an alarm in my holy mountain: let all the inhabitants of the land tremble: for the day of the Lord cometh, for it is nigh at hand. (Joel 2:1) *For a nation is come upon my land, strong, and without number . . . a great people and a strong; there hath not been ever the like, neither shall be any more after it, even to the years of many generations.* (Joel 1:6, 2:2)

The time has come to 'sound the alarm'. It is time to 'sound the trumpet' loud and clear throughout the length and breadth of Britain.

For Britain today is fast heading towards a grievous peril, the like of which she has never experienced before. Like some great ship at sea on a collision course with icebergs, and with both her radio and radar switched off, she has been ignoring all the warnings sent, has already passed all the danger signals, and is moving quickly towards a disaster of truly titanic and world-shattering proportions.

Yet her people 'soldier on', blissfully unaware, it would seem, that they are in any danger at all.

We, in Britain, have become a race of ostriches with heads deeply buried in the sand, quite oblivious of what is going on around us, let alone of the extreme danger which

98

is fast appearing over the horizon. And it is high time to set all the alarm bells ringing.

When I felt the burden of the Lord to issue *A Warning to the Nation* in 1969, I did so because I could see quite clearly that Britain had passed from the position of being a nation which had experienced the hand of Almighty God in *blessing* – all down the years of her history and in remarkable deliverances – to becoming a nation under God's *judgments*, because of the way she had forsaken God and was now deliberately flying in his face.

I also warned at that time that unless Britain repents and returns to the Lord, there is an even worse judgment to come. We need to wake up to the fact that the judgments of God are progressive in character and in severity, and that this is particularly so when gross sin and wickedness are on the increase and continue to remain largely unchecked.

The Bible clearly shows that when one form of judgment fails to bring a people to repentance, God has to visit them with another judgment – of a more severe kind. And often he has to continue with another, and yet another. Each visitation takes a more serious form than the previous one, whilst all the time God is pleading with his people to return to him.

When the leaders and people of a nation, such as our own, stubbornly refuse to heed the warnings which have repeatedly been given and deliberately choose to ignore the many signs which God has been doing amongst them, then God has to resort to far more stringent methods in order to bring such a people to its knees. And if there is still no sign of repentance when he has done that, the Bible clearly teaches that as iniquity in the nation comes to the full, there has to come a day of final reckoning.

Indeed, there has to come the time when, just as in the days of Noah, the storm must finally break; or as in the days of Sodom and Gomorrah, the fire and brimstone must come down from heaven; or as in the days of

Jeremiah, the enemy armies must overrun the land.

To me, that day seems perilously near for Britain.

For the lesson that needs to be understood in this country is that if we will not learn any other way, then we must expect to have to learn the hard way. That means having to experience the very severest type of God's judgments.

And it seems to me, that this is what we are about to see happening to us.

I was really forced to sit up and take notice when I discovered, whilst reading my Bible during the summer of 1976 – the year of the great drought – that the kind of drought which we were then experiencing was, in the days of the prophets Joel and Jeremiah, the precursor of a judgment at the hands of an invading enemy army. The very severe and unusual drought in their day was God switching on the danger lights. It was the harbinger of a far greater evil to follow. It was God's way of setting all the alarm bells ringing – God's way of waking everybody up!

In Jeremiah's case, the judgment at the hands of an invading enemy army followed hard on the heels of judgment by a very serious drought. On the other hand, in Joel's case they practically coincided with each other.

That discovery really worried me then. And it still does, especially when I realise that Britain's great coming day of judgment may only have been delayed temporarily.

Look at what we have done to contribute to our own national landslide, and so to make such a day a terrible possibility. For years we have permitted the whittling away of the nation's Christian foundations until now there is very little of them left. Belief in God has been largely overthrown, together with any belief in the authority of the Bible and of the *whole* of the Bible.

Consequently, our people are no longer being taught that each person will have to give an account to God at the day of judgment for the kind of life he or she has lived;

that there is such a thing as an after life; that there are such places as heaven and hell; and that a man will ultimately spend the whole of eternity in one or the other, depending on whether or not he accepts the Lord Jesus Christ as his own personal Saviour, and as the *only way* of salvation.

The result of all this is that people now live just as they please, with no fear of God before their eyes. All Christian principles and standards have been largely rejected, and have been replaced by loose-living, promiscuity, free-love, dishonesty and deception. The long-accepted standards of truth, virtue, uprightness, nobility, decency and pureness of living have not only been allowed to become outmoded, but to be regarded as things now to be treated with utter derision, to be despised, scorned and mocked at, and finally to be swept utterly away.

With all such restraints and restrictions removed, we have allowed the flood-gates of a great cesspool of iniquity to be thrown wide open, permitting the foul, stinking, sewage-waters of corruption, pornography, immorality, depravity, perversion and decay to surge in and engulf our land. And God is extremely angry on account of this – make no mistake about it. The fire of his fierce wrath has been mightily aroused against us as a nation.

With our moral and spiritual defences down, we have permitted the run-down of the nation's defences to such a degree that Britain is left more vulnerable now than at any time in her long history, whilst all the time the Soviet and Warsaw Pact forces have been building up their military, naval and air strengths alarmingly.

In doing all this, we have been sowing within the nation, and within ourselves, the seeds of our own destruction. And in the process we have created the ideal situation for a Communist take-over, both from within the nation and from without. So let us be quite clear. Were that take-over to happen, it should be interpreted as a judgment of God upon us for all this blatant wickedness.

Britain urgently needs a prophet today. Even secular magazines have frequently expressed this sentiment. More than one of them, in reviewing some aspect or other of our national situation, has said: 'Is there no voice of the prophet to be heard in the land?'

Yes, Britain desperately needs a prophet today. If ever there was a time when our nation needed such a challenging ministry, it is now. And were God to send us such a prophet, I am sure the first thing he would be heard to say is this: 'Britain, you have gone exactly the same way that Israel in the Old Testament went; and because of this, you are suffering the same consequences. *That* is the explanation of all that you see happening to you at the present moment.'

And I am sure he would add: 'Britain, if you still refuse to repent and turn to the Lord your God, despite all that you have been experiencing by way of divine chastisements, you are likely to suffer the same consequences that Israel in the Old Testament eventually suffered, which, I would remind you, was destruction at the hands of an invading enemy.'

Such a prophet might also be heard to say, as Haggai and Amos said in their day: 'Thus saith the Lord concerning Britain, consider your ways. Ye have sown much and bring in little; and he that earneth wages, earneth wages to put it into a bag with holes, and yet ye have not returned unto me', saith the Lord.

'Ye looked for much, and lo, it came to little; and when ye brought it home, I did blow upon it, and yet ye have not returned unto me,' saith the Lord.

'I have smitten your fields with blasting and with mildew, and when the crops of your corn-fields, your vegetable plots and your fruit orchards increased, I sent the aphids, the whitefly and the greenfly to destroy them, and yet ye have not returned unto me, saith the Lord.

'I called for a drought upon the land, and caused the heaven over you to be stayed for dew, and the earth to be stayed from her fruit, and yet ye did not return unto me, saith the Lord.

'I have caused fierce fires to ravage your woodlands, heaths and forests, and yet ye have not returned unto me, saith the Lord.

'I have sent pestilence and disease to your farmsteads, the foot and mouth disease amongst your cattle, the swine-vesicular disease amongst your pigs, the fowl-pest to ravage your chicken and pheasant runs, the wool disease amongst your sheep, and yet ye have not returned unto me, saith the Lord.

'I have withheld success from your factories, causing your national production to fall off, and I called for the curtailing of your oil supplies, and yet ye have not returned unto me, saith the Lord.

'I have even brought you teetering on the brink of financial and economic ruin, so that you did not know which way to turn for financial assistance, and even then ye have not returned unto me, saith the Lord.

'Therefore, thus will I do unto thee, O Britain; and because of what I am about to do unto thee, prepare for what is about to come upon you, O proud and stubborn kingdom situated in the midst of the North Sea.'

The prophet in the Old Testament was also called a seer, because he was endowed by God with a special gift of perception which enabled him to see very clearly what was coming.

I believe that such a prophet would then be heard crying out: 'Blow ye the trumpet in the land, and sound the alarm throughout the length and breadth of Britain; let all the inhabitants of the land *tremble; for, for you, O people of Britain, the day of the Lord cometh;* for it is nigh at hand.'

I believe his message would be strikingly similar to that of the prophet Jeremiah and, like Jeremiah, he would give warning of the danger which he could see approaching: *Blow the trumpet in Tekoa . . . for evil appeareth out of the north, and great destruction.* (Jeremiah 6:1) *The lion (or bear) is come up from the thicket, and the destroyer of the Gentiles is on his way; he is gone forth from his place to make thy land desolate* (Jeremiah 4:7).

And I believe his message would be remarkably like that of the prophet Joel: *Blow ye the trumpet in Zion... sound an alarm...For a nation is come up upon my land, strong, and without number . . . a great people and a strong; there hath not been ever the like, neither shall be any more after it, even to the years of many generations.* (Joel 2:1, 1:6, 2:2)

This is what these two prophets were heard saying in *their* day, and they were proclaiming it in the wake of a very severe and unusual drought. When we consider all the grave warnings that leading military authorities in the West have been issuing about the alarming size of the Soviet build-up in recent years, who can afford to say that judgment such as Jeremiah and Joel were warning their people about, is not a possibility today?

We are told, for instance, that the Soviets have at their disposal 2½ million Warsaw Pact troops; well over 45,000 Soviet tanks; over 10,000 aircraft; 2,000 or more inter-continental ballistic missiles; over 4,000 missile nuclear warheads; 10,000 anti-aircraft missile strategic launchers; and that they have ten times more submarines than Hitler had at the start of the 1939 War, some 80 of which are driven by nuclear power, and some 50 of which are nuclear-powered strategic missile-launching platforms. In addition, they are launching one new nuclear-powered tactical submarine *every month*.

This vast build-up of Soviet military might has been going on for years, despite the fact that our political leaders, who have been drastically reducing our own defence forces, know quite well that Kruschev once said: 'When their guard is down, we will smash them.' And the question which needs increasingly to be asked is: Why?

What is the intention of this phenomenal build-up?

General Sir Walter Walker, formerly NATO Commander-in-Chief, Allied Forces, Northern Europe, has written: 'The Kremlin has embarked on a massive armaments build-up without parallel in history. This concentration of military strength far exceeds any conceivable requirement for the Soviet's own defence, and can only have the most ominous implications for the West. The Warsaw Pact now outnumbers NATO in every conceivable category of weapons system on the central front in Europe.'

Dr James Schlesinger, former Defence Secretary of the United States, says that the total picture is of a Soviet force-structure twice NATO's in ground power and essentially twice NATO's in air power. It has in fact been revealed that the Russians have built up an army three times larger than America's, with almost five times as many tanks, six times the artillery, and more than double the number of personnel-carriers. Defence planners in Washington are deeply concerned, if not downright alarmed, by the realisation that the Russians will very soon achieve nuclear parity with them – if they have not done so already.

Again the question inevitably arises in any logically-thinking mind: Why? *Why* are they persistently seeking to overhaul the West in this way?

The then supreme Allied Commander in Europe, General Alexander Haig, said as far back as November 1976: 'A dangerous situation exists in which a blatant crossing of the frontiers in Central Europe is a possibility.'

And General Sir Walter Walker has put it this way: 'This vast Soviet military machine is designed specifically to launch a massive, surprise, *blitzkrieg* attack – without prior concentration of forces, and possibly under the guise of manoeuvres and exercises – aimed at advancing at lightning speed at the rate of 70 miles per day, and at the same time blinding our own forces with their electronic warfare capability.

'They would crunch their way forward, regardless of casualties, at this speed of 70 miles per day, supported in depth by airborne troops, armed helicopters, air attack, amphibious attack on the flanks, and chemical attack. And this rate of advance, so far as Western Europe is concerned, would bring them to the Rhine in less than 48 hours and to the Channel ports in less than a week.

'The speed, devasting power, and velocity of the Soviet onslaught would be such, that NATO would not be able to resort to the use of their tactical nuclear weapons, for the simple reason that there would not be sufficient time for the necessary political decisions to be taken. In any case, the missile sites would already have been overrun. It would be surprising if the Soviet General Staff did not know the number and location of every nuclear bomb site in Western Europe.'

Meanwhile, the Soviet surface and underwater fleet is now so strong and powerful that they are in a position to cut all our main shipping routes at sea almost anywhere in the world.

In late January 1976, Dr Schlesinger issued this grave warning: 'At no point since the 1930s has the western world faced so formidable a threat to its survival.' And General Sir Walter Walker said in the same month: 'Never has the situation in Europe been so grave. The free world stands today in greater peril than at any time since the dark days of the Second World War. And yet from Western Europe, clarion call comes there none.'

Or again, more recently: 'Is there no voice among free men, apart from Solzhenitsyn and Mrs Margaret Thatcher – is there no one else in Western Europe who will sound the alarm as Churchill did before the war?'

So who can possibly afford to bury their heads in the sand? Isn't it time to 'sound the alarm'? I wrote in *A Warning to the Nation*: 'If Sir Winston Churchill had been alive today, he would have raised the alarm long ago.

Britain is more vulnerable now than she was just after Dunkirk.'

But that was in 1969. The situation now is far more serious than it was then. It is even far more serious than it was in 1939 because Britain is in far graver danger.

At that time there were tiny forces at work in this country who were in league with Hitler and his Nazi regime, whereas today there are powerful and treacherous forces in the country at work and in league with Communist Russia, waiting to help effect a take-over when they see the time is ripe to do so.

I am a preacher. And as a preacher, I am deeply concerned with the *spiritual* implications of all this, for the spiritual implications rate far higher in priority than do even the military implications.

When the grave peril, which is without question confronting Britain today, can be interpreted as possibly the next form of judgment with which God will have to visit Britain – then, I say, it is high time to *sound the trumpet and warn the people.*

The trumpet needs to be sounded loud and clear.

It should be sounded out from the roof-tops and from every high hill.

It should be sounded forth in every road and street in Britain.

It should be sounded in all Britain's towns and villages.

It should be sounded in every church, chapel, and meeting-hall in the land.

It should be sounded down the central aisle of every cathedral.

It should be sounded in all our big cities.

It should be sounded in every factory and workshop.

It should be sounded loud and clear, up and down Fleet Street.

Its long resounding notes should be sent reverberating down all the corridors of power within the Palace of Westminster.

It should be sounded outside number 10 Downing Street, in the cabinet room, and in the Treasury.

It should be sounded all down Whitehall and outside Transport House.

It should be sounded loud and clear both outside and inside Buckingham Palace.

It should be sounded to warn the people of a fast approaching day of God in judgment for Britain.

It should be sounded forth to tell them of the urgent need to repent, to turn from their sins, and to get right with God by seeking forgiveness and cleansing in the precious blood of Jesus Christ, lest that day come upon them unawares. For that is why the prophets sounded the trumpet in the days of the Old Testament. They saw clearly what was coming, so they gave out the warning – particularly that men and women should repent and put far from them all their sins, and get right with God.

What we need to see, above all, is that in Jeremiah's and Joel's day God dealt with these wilfully unrepentant people of Israel so severely that he literally brought them, crying out to him in desperation, to their knees. If a people will not learn any *other* way, then they have to learn the hard way, in terms of the very severest forms of the judgments of God.

The coming day of God in Joel's time was so terrible that God commanded his prophet to assemble all the inhabitants of the land into the house of the Lord their God with a long blast of the trumpet, together with their elders and their rulers – every one without exception. It was to be thorough – babes in arms, children, young people just about to get married – everyone!

When he had gathered them all into the house of the Lord, God told Joel that he was to tell the priests and ministers to literally 'cry unto the Lord' – 'to howl', God said, with great tears. And with the enemy streaming across their borders (Joel 2:3-11) and practically on the steps of where they were assembled, they were to cry out: *Spare thy people, O Lord, and give not thine heritage to reproach, that the heathen should rule over them: wherefore should they say among the people, Where is their God?* (Joel 2:17)

In other words, with the enemy already at the gates, the prophet Joel was told by God to call the nation together for an urgent time of repentance and prayer.

Please note that, archbishops and other church leaders in Britain. Days and periods of national prayer and repentance are scriptural! It was God himself who commanded that this one should be called; he did not wait for the leaders of the national church to call one, or for government officials to authorise it, because it would never have happened. No – he used a prophet in the nation to bring it about, and that prophet took complete charge of the national situation.

Even 'the powers that be' had to do what he said, and rally into the house of the Lord! With the enemy rapidly overrunning the land, God said to all those whom he was assembling together: *Therefore also now, saith the Lord, turn ye even to me with all your heart, and with fasting, and with weeping, and with mourning: and rend your heart, and not your garments, and turn unto the Lord your God: for he is gracious and merciful, slow to anger, and of great kindness, and repenteth him of the evil. Who knoweth if he will return and repent, and leave a blessing behind him?* (Joel 2:12-14)

And look what God promised to do as a result of their obedience: *Then will the Lord be jealous for his land, and pity his people. Yea, the Lord will answer . . .* (Joel 2:18-19).

The following verses tell *how* he will answer.

First, he will reverse all the effects of the drought: *Behold, I will send you corn, and wine, and oil, and ye shall be satisfied therewith* (Joel 2:19).

Second, he will drive out the invader: *I will remove far off from you the northern army, and will drive him into a land barren and desolate, with his face towards the east sea*

(Joel 2:20).

Third, he will restore to them their former prosperity: *Fear not, O land; be glad and rejoice: for the Lord will do great things . . .*

And the floors shall be full of wheat, and the vats shall overflow with wine and oil.

And I will restore to you the years that the locust hath eaten, the cankerworm, and the caterpillar, and the palmerworm, my great army which I sent among you.

And ye shall eat in plenty, and be satisfied, and praise the name of the Lord your God, that hath dealt wondrously with you: and my people shall never be ashamed.

And ye shall know that I am in the midst of Israel, and that I am the Lord your God, and none else: and my people shall never be ashamed. (Joel 2:21-7)

Fourth, he will visit them with a great spiritual revival – a Pentecost!

And it shall come to pass afterward, that I will pour out my spirit upon all flesh; and your sons and your daughters shall prophesy, your old men shall dream dreams, your young men shall see visions; and also upon the servants and upon the handmaids in those days will I pour out my spirit. (Joel 2:28,29)

That was the pathway to national restoration and spiritual revival in those days. It is also the pathway to national restoration and spiritual revival today. When will we learn that the way ahead for Britian is *not* by borrowing more millions from the International Monetary Fund; *not* by forming a coalition government; *not* by relying on North Sea oil or by any other man-made solution. It is by crying out to Almighty God for deliverance on our knees in humble repentance.

That was why Joel's trumpet call was sounded; and the trumpet needs to be sounded in just the same way for Britain today. Because Britain has departed from the Lord, and sinned so grievously against him, there is an equally fearful day of judgment coming upon her if she still persists in not repenting and returning to the Lord her

God. And if that judgment comes, I fear it is likely to be extremely severe, and exceedingly terrible.

Chapter Nine
What is Really Wrong with Britain?

The Secular Answer

Now I am well aware that this is a devastatingly strong statement to make. In what sense, then, can it be said to be true? To get at the answer, certain other questions need to be raised: 'What is really wrong with Britain?' and 'Why is she in such a mess?'

It is time we got down to making a thorough and drastic diagnosis of Britain's tragically sick condition in order to discover what is *basically* wrong with this once great nation. In other words, we need to get at the root cause of all our troubles; to see why it is that we have gone to pieces so quickly. If you like, we need to discover what is at the very heart of it all.

Any doctor will tell you that it is no use whatsoever treating the symptoms of a disease – the spots that appear on the skin, or the boils that break out, first in one part of the body and then in another – until he has thoroughly investigated what is causing these symptoms to appear. It is when he has discovered that, and only then, that he can pronounce and begin to apply the cure.

So it is with a nation. Several attempts have been made in recent years to answer our questions, but none of them ever seems to get down deep enough, to get to the heart of the matter. Consequently the findings and conclusions reached tend to be very superficial, even pathetically naive at times.

During the last two years, for instance, a series of articles has been running in one of our leading national newspapers and raising the question: What is wrong with Britain? Some fifteen leading statesmen, scientists, university professors, business magnates and journalists of this and other countries all made contributions to this series.

One of the early contributors said quite rightly: 'Some Gibbon, from a vantage point in the future, will no doubt write of "The Decline and Fall of Great Britain and the British Empire".' He continued: 'In the life-span of some of us still alive, Great Britain has fallen, rung by rung, from a pre-eminent position in both political and industrial fields to second- or even third-rate status.' (And it is very significant indeed that he did not even mention how Britain has fallen from a pre-eminent position in the spiritual and moral realm as well. This dimension of things never seems to come into such people's estimations or calculations. And yet it is *here* that the real answer lies.)

All the contributors reached various conclusions as to what is wrong with our country, but only one of them ever got any deeper than the economic, industrial, political, or social level.

Their conclusions can be summarised in this way: Britain's troubles stem from two world wars; from the destruction of wealth which resulted from these two wars; from the loss of her empire. What is wrong is Britain's *class*-structure. The problem is nothing more than economic – nothing which cannot be cured by mastering inflation, sharply reducing our balance of payments, and becoming self-sufficient in oil. The trouble is due to the Arabs quadrupling the price of oil. It is all due to a faulty system of education; to a failure to train the rising generation for jobs, crafts, and professions where they are most needed. The troubles stem from the desire to consume socially what is not being produced individually; from faulty processes of natural wealth-production and from failure to use the wealth-producing regulator rightly. What is wrong is the intolerable strain which is being imposed on Britain's parliamentary system at the present time. The trouble with Britain is that too much is expected of her! Why should any country continue to be for ever great?

I would suggest that to come to such conclusions is only scratching at the surface. It is merely looking at the symptoms all the time, not at the root cause.

Of all the contributors, Lord Hailsham was the only one who went anywhere near deep enough: 'The cause of our troubles is not economic, nor has it anything to do with world conditions or our loss of Empire, nor with any of the other easy excuses which we are so ready to accept and which our present rulers invent for our comfort. *It is a disease of the spirit* from which there is no one to blame but ourselves.' (my italics)

He warned that in his view the country will only begin to return to sanity by learning the hard way, and this, he said, 'will mean widespread unemployment and financial ruin . . . I do not believe that these catastrophes are far off.'

This was coming much nearer to the truth. But when he began to point to the way out of our malaise, I was not sure whether he meant that we could save the situation by our own self-effort.

Such, then, was the result of the attempt through this series of articles to get at the root of Britain's troubles.

Then the House of Lords conducted a five-and-a half-hour debate about the state of the nation on 14 July 1976. During that debate the same issue was being considered, but in the form of the following question: What has happened in this country in the thirty years since the war, which has caused such a steady decline?

No less than twenty-one peers took part. Lord

Carrington, who opened the debate, categorically stated that nobody could deny that the state of the nation was critical, economically and socially (although, once again, no mention was made, at this stage, of our state *spiritually*). Other speakers said that an overwhelming number of people in this country knew that something was wrong, and that somewhere along the lines over these last twenty-five years or so, the rot in our social fabric has worsened until today we face the question which has faced so many civilisations before. Corruption, and not just bribery and corruption, is there in many areas of our national life for anyone with eyes to see, so that the search for the answer right now as to whether this corruption in our society is curable is more than somewhat urgent.

Yet, despite all this, I was shattered to discover that more than one peer was naive enough to say that there is nothing inherently wrong with our society; that although we have our little malaise periodically – and we are in the midst of a malaise at this moment – there is not really much wrong with us; things are really no different from what they have ever been. And 'I do not believe that the United Kingdom is in any way as bad as some feel that it is.'

True, another did urge obliquely that 'a diagnosis of the state of the nation was necessary.' And yet another said strongly that 'we ought to recognise where we have gone wrong.' But when it came to making that diagnosis, once again the probing did not go anywhere near deep enough.

Some of the speeches made this abundantly clear. They can be summarised in this way: The trouble is due to our present form of Government; to the need for electoral reform; to the fact that power is slipping away from Parliament. One of the many elements in the decline is the malfunction of the constitution. Our problems are due to the fact that many countries in the world have lost faith in Britain. The trouble comes from having tried since the war to do too much and to expect too much from our economic system; from the failure of men and machines to come to terms with themselves. A great deal of the fault lies in industry; the problems facing us now can be seen in economic terms, in terms of greed. What has brought us into the humiliating position in which we find ourselves today is the combination of two clear and different tendencies: one, a greater rate of inflation than elsewhere in the world, and, two, our productivity has been so comparatively low.

A few speakers got nearer to the truth when they said that 'there has been a widespread and continuing decline in organised Christianity in these islands. Having lost that faith . . . we have not found anything comparable to put in its place.' (As if that is possible!) This speaker added: 'We are living in a secular age, and we are reaping the results of that secularity.'

Another speaker commented: 'The biggest and most important change which has vitally concerned everything since the 1930s because of its enormous effect on personal attitudes, is that religion no longer provides the yardstick by which people's behaviour was directly or indirectly influenced. At the same time, the largely accepted, relatively stable order of society which we inherited from the Victorians has passed away. In place of religion, with a belief in an after-life, a humanistic approach has to some extent taken over.'

Lord Home, in an excellent speech, said, 'There is evidence that faith in the essential Christian foundations of our society is faltering. Why do the young not rally to the Christian standard as their forefathers did?'

These speakers lifted the debate on to a higher plane and were probing in the right direction for the root cause of what was wrong. But they were still not going far enough, or digging anywhere near deep enough. For instance, I searched through the whole set of twenty-one speeches in vain for any reference to Almighty God, or to the nation's relationship with him.

The debate was brought to an appalling anti-climax when a closing speaker said: 'The real issue is the economic decline. The pound sterling has been declining for at least fifty years. It has been a continual decline. But the oil which is to be found in the North Sea and in other parts surrounding our coasts, provides us with a real opportunity to put our house in order.' (Would you believe it?)

When I read that, my heart sank into my boots. How pathetic! How blind can a man be? How materialistic can he get? And so the debate closed without ever really getting to the real root of the trouble.

What is needed, therefore, is a far more drastic and radical enquiry into what really is wrong with Britain than was provided by these two investigations, or by any other that I have seen so far.

Chapter Ten
What is Really Wrong with Britain?

The Biblical Answer

What then is the *heart* of the matter? What is really wrong with Britain?

In the first place, the Bible makes it very plain that most of our troubles, both personal and national, are due to the fact that *we, as a people, are living without God.* We do not relate to him in any way. We are not in touch with him. We do not bring matters to him in prayer. This explains why things are going the way that they are; why we, as a nation, and as individuals, are going the way that we are. And I find that this is gradually beginning to dawn on people.

For instance, as I got into an Underground train a short time ago, a Christian man whom I had not seen for a number of years, sat down next to me and said, 'Mr Gardner, my eldest daughter has just taken up teaching in school, and she says it is chaos! – literally chaos! What advice would you give her as to how she can gain some sort of control, when few or no corrective measures are allowed to be introduced today?'

I replied: 'It is not so much the advice I would give *her*, as the advice which all of us need to be given all over again, and that is, that *God* has shown us the principles of bringing up children – whether we are parents, school teachers, youth leaders, Bible class leaders or whatever.

And until we get back to those principles, we shall never get anywhere. God says, 'Train up the child in the way he should go' (Proverbs 22:6). Train him up!

'Training involves discipline, and discipline includes correction. Sometimes it also involves chastisement, and the Bible has a lot to say about chastisement.'

He said, 'Yes, I know. But we are not allowed to do that now.'

I replied: 'It is because we have abandoned these principles which God has given us, that we are reaping the fruits of that abandonment – in terms of chaos in schools, vandalism in public places, riots in the streets, and terrorism and hooliganism on the football terraces. In fact, I believe that the words of the second commandment are terribly applicable today, when God said that the sins of the fathers would be visited upon the children 'unto the third and fourth generation of them that hate me', but that he would show mercy 'unto thousands of them that love me and keep my commandments.' (Exodus 20:5,6) I am obliged to ask: Is a lot of what we see going on in this realm of the nation's children and young people, fulfilment of what God says would happen – 'visiting the iniquity of the fathers upon the children' – for our lack of disciplining them and following the principles of bringing up children which God has outlined in the Bible? The lesson is clear. Abandon these principles and you inevitably suffer the consequences.'

My friend went on to lament the fact that the ten commandments are no longer taught in schools. He said, 'They are not even taught in churches or in the Sunday schools.' And he added, 'Christianity isn't being taught in schools any longer, either. My younger boys are being taught about Buddhism, Hinduism, and Islam – not about Christianity. The result is that they are totally confused. And I brought them up to believe in the Lord Jesus Christ! It seems that we have thrown teaching about God, about Christianity, about Christian standards, about the

Bible, completely overboard – and *what is there left?*'

'Yes', I said. 'So long as we continue to disregard all these things, matters will get worse, not better.'

The Bible says, 'Cursed be he that removeth his neighbour's landmark.' (Deuteronomy 27:17) My fear is that this is what God has caused to be written in large letters over many of our churches, over schools, over our entire educational system, and indeed over Britain's parliament. And I believe that much of what we are experiencing in our nation today is because we have come under that curse. I repeat, we are a nation and a people which is living without God. And that, basically, is *one of the root causes of our troubles.*

*   *   *   *

As if living without God is not serious enough, my reading of the Bible shows me very clearly, in the second place, that *we are defying him openly, and are deliberately going against him.* I believe that to be the next part of the answer as to what is basically wrong with Britain.

During the last ten years or more, we have so reversed our country's laws and changed our moral and spiritual direction, that we have become a nation which has put itself on a direct collision course with God. And because we have, we have been bringing down God's judgments upon us. Now that is a pretty devastating claim to make. How do we establish that it is true, and that this is indeed what is happening?

Surely the answer is that we should examine the position in the light of all that is put to us in the Bible, and apply to our situation what is so clearly revealed to us there. We shall then be left in no doubt whatsoever. And one of the best places in the Bible from which to do that, is Deutronomy chapter 28.

There are at least thirty judgments mentioned in this chapter which can come upon a nation because God is against it, and, in my opinion, Britain has already experienced twenty-seven of them. The remaining three could come upon her at any moment. Indeed, Deuteronomy 28:46 says of these judgments: 'And they shall be upon you for a sign' – for a sign that God is against you. And certainly for a sign that you are going against him.

The deeply disturbing fact is that a whole host of these things has been happening to Britain for some time, giving evidence enough to establish that we are indeed a nation on a collision course with God.

Take, for example, the first few of the judgments mentioned between verses 15 and 20 of Deuteronomy 28.

1) *Cursed shalt thou be in the city*. (v 16) In a modern age, that is the place where the money is made. Or lost! The city – it speaks to us of everything in the realm of finance, or in the realm of the national economy. And look what has been happening to our economy in recent years!

Our entire financial and economic system seems to be under a curse. 'Cursed shalt thou be in the city': it has been happening.

2) *And cursed shalt thou be in the field*. (v 16) The unusually prolonged winter of 1979 was surely a sign of the judgments of God upon us. But for a number of years now we have been experiencing very unusual weather conditions.

For instance, in 1978, early spring crops were held back by the persistently cold, dull weather, and there was so much torrential rain that farmers were reporting whole acres of seed just rotting in the ground. On the other hand, in 1974, soon after much of the seed had been sown in the earlier part of the year, we had an unusually dry spell. The result was that much of the seed just did not germinate. So large areas of farmland had to be re-sown. Then in the beginning of September 1974, all the national newspapers confidently boasted that there was the promise of a bumper harvest. But what happened?

On a number of occasions, the British Isles were

severely shaken and buffeted by unusually severe storms. Strong gales, and winds of hurricane force, swept through the country, wreaking untold havoc and laying much of the corn; added to which the whole of the British Isles were subjected to torrential rains. The wet weather so persisted that it was impossible to lift the sugar beet crop out of the ground, or to take lorries on to the fields to carry it away. Consequently some sugar beet factories had to close down. Then in December 1974 the fields were so wet and sodden that in many areas the potato crop was still in the ground because it was impossible to lift it.

In 1976, there was the prolonged drought which, according to the *Daily Telegraph's* agricultural correspondent, gave the country its worst grain harvest for six years, and also added at least £80 million to the nation's import bill. But the drought also seriously affected the root crops, which shrivelled for lack of moisture. The pea-crop in many areas did not even come up! Milk yields were quite seriously affected, due to the scarcity of grass for the cow-herds.

This kind of thing has been going on for a number of years now. 'Cursed shalt thou be in the field.' And we *have* been.

3) *Cursed shall be thy basket and thy store.* (v 17) That means 'shopping basket' in a modern age, housewives! And it means store-cupboards and larders, anxious mothers – with all the constantly soaring prices in mind, increasing alarmingly almost every week, and with the food supplies in the store-cupboards forever running out. 'Cursed shall be thy basket and thy store.'

4) *Cursed shall be the fruit of thy body.* (v 18) That means your children, people of Britain! I have already referred to this in terms of chaos in our schools, vandalism and terrorism in our streets, and hooliganism on the football terraces. To all that must be added the appalling crime-rate amongst children, even little children, and young people. The national crime statistical reports show that

five-year-olds are now well and truly involved.

What we are seeing is a generation gone wild; a generation almost totally beyond control. 'Cursed shall be the fruit of thy body' – thy children. It is *happening* in the nation. Who cannot say that, somehow, so many of those who have gone wild seem to be under some kind of a curse?

And while we are still dealing with things in the domestic realm, verse 30 says: 'Thou shalt betroth a wife, and another man shall lie with her.' Isn't that happening too, in our homes? Unfaithfulness of husbands and wives on a frightening scale is reflected in the ever-increasing divorce rate; and now there is the appallingly wide-spread practice of husband- and wife-swapping. In terms of such judgments in the domestic realm, family life and homes all over the country seem indeed to be sorely smitten.

5) *Cursed shall be . . . the fruit of thy land.* (v 18) This verse, when linked with such statements as those in verses 30, 39 and 40, obviously includes the fruit of the trees – fruit trees or orchards. For verse 30 says: 'Thou shalt plant a vineyard [or orchard] and shalt not gather the grapes thereof', whilst verse 39 adds 'for the worms [or maggots] shall eat them.' And verse 40: 'Thou shalt have olive trees throughout all thy coasts, but thou shalt not anoint thyself with oil; for thine olive shall cast his fruit [that means drop off].'

This kind of thing has been happening in our English orchards and gardens. We have seen it with heavily laden pear trees. Before the pears had time to grow to their full size, suddenly their stems began to wilt, wither away and decay, and hundreds of the half-formed fruit began falling and littering the ground. The pears, if not the olives, were seen to be casting their fruit. Then just as the remaining fruit was ripening it was discovered that practically every one had a maggot inside! That verse could equally well read: 'Thou shalt plant a fruit orchard and shalt not gather the fruit thereof for the maggots shall eat them.'

We have seen it happen with apples, too; on numerous occasions, thousands of tons of apples have gone to waste, either because they were not fit for marketing, or because there was not the labour available to gather them. 'Thou shalt plant orchards but thou shalt not eat the fruit thereof . . . Cursed shall be the fruit of thy land.'

6) *Cursed shall be . . . the increase of thy kine* [or cattle], *and the flocks of thy sheep.* (v 18) We have already seen in *A Warning to the Nation* what was happening towards the end of 1967. Foot and mouth disease had begun to rage amongst the cattle until it reached the dimensions of a national disaster.

'Thine ox [cattle] shall be slain before thine eyes, and thou shalt not eat thereof' (v 31). Which is exactly what has to happen as a result of foot and mouth disease, isn't it? Our cattle had to be slain before our eyes, and we could not eat them.

Since then, swine vesicular disease began to break out and spread alarmingly, until in a period of four years there had been nearly 400 outbreaks, involving the slaughter of 204,000 pigs. And it cost the taxpayer nearly £8 million in a four-year fight to stamp it out. Then in January 1973, a highly contagious disease amongst sheep suddenly reappeared, seriously affecting the wool-crop.

What has happened since then? In 1975, farmers all over the country were not able to get the necessary feeding stuffs with which to feed their livestock; cows, calves and beef-cattle had to be slaughtered in vast quantities.

In 1976, because of the severe drought, the same thing had to happen. Cattle and livestock had to be slaughtered on a quite frightening scale. 'Your cattle shall be slain before your eyes, and you shall not eat of it.' And it has been happening in Britain ever since 1967. 'Cursed shall be . . . the increase of thy kine, [cattle] and the flocks of thy sheep.'

What we see happening here, is surely not just a *single* judgment of God, but part of a long process of judgments which has been taking place in this country for at least ten years now. God says in Deuteronomy 28:20 that it is 'because of the wickedness of thy doings, whereby thou hast forsaken me.' *That* is the reason. Cannot anybody recognise the signs?

While we are still dealing with agriculture, let me point out that Deutronomy 28:31 also says: 'Thine ass shall be violently taken away from before thy face, and shall not be restored unto thee.' And this has been happening too.

Since *A Warning to the Nation* was first published, the National Farmers Union has had to issue an urgent warning to farmers to brand their cattle, because of a widespread outbreak of night-rustling in cattle-rearing and horse-breeding districts. One report said that many thousands of pounds worth of horses and cattle have been herded away in night raids, and have disappeared without trace. Farmers in Devon, Cornwall, Surrey, Sussex, East Anglia and Yorkshire have reported serious losses. We have only to change the wording of that verse very slightly to read 'Your *horses* and your cattle shall be violently taken away from under your very noses, and shall not be restored to you', and you have a most graphic description of what is actually taking place on many a farm in Britain today. Horses and cattle disappear without trace; not to mention deer in the New Forest.

And in case any farmer should be tempted to say: 'Oh, we are alright. Our farm is 100 per cent mechanised', let me tell him that tractors are now disappearing overnight without trace – not just horses!

7) *The Lord shall send upon thee cursing, vexation [frustration in the RSV] and rebuke, in all that thou settest thine hand unto, for to do, until thou be destroyed, and until thou perish quickly; because of the wickedness of thy doings, whereby thou hast forsaken me.* (v 20) Coupled with that, God says in verse 29, 'And thou shalt not prosper in thy ways'.

The phrase 'in all that thou settest thine hand unto, for

to do', involves pretty well everything that you could mention in any sphere. And it certainly covers everything that has to do with a nation's industry, with its produce-making and wealth-creating processes. Isn't this exactly what has been happening, and is happening, in the nation's industrial realm? No progress is being made any-where for long.

In that debate on the state of the nation held in the House of Lords, Lord Byers said: 'As compared with our competitors abroad . . . [and he instanced West Germany in particular] the most remarkable thing about the United Kingdom industry over the last twenty-five years has been *the speed of its relative decline.'* (my italics) But nobody ever seems to ask 'Why?'. And Lord Robbins, during the same debate, referred to 'this humiliating position in which we find ourselves today.'

But this has been our position for quite a long time now. It is at least nine years since Prince Philip said, concerning our industry: 'I do not think anyone can claim that Britain's record has been wholly successful during the last twenty years. Many things have gone wrong.'

First came the shattering news that Rolls-Royce had collapsed. That really shook the country. It also shook the United States of America. Indeed it shook the whole world.

Soon after that, we saw the second largest car assurance company go into liquidation. Then came the collapse of Chrysler; followed by Nortons. British Leyland got into serious trouble, and the Government had to 'bale them out'. Next we saw the British postal service beginning to deteriorate, with postal charges rising higher and higher for fewer and less efficient services. Then British Rail got into difficulties and began to be referred to in the Press as 'Bankrupt British Rail'. In the whole realm of British industry we see 'frustration', 'confusion', 'vexation' and 'delays' in all that we, as a nation, 'set our hand unto for to do'. Britain, today, is indeed a frustrated nation. In fact, the Earl of Gowrie said during that same debate in the House of Lords: 'If I had to sum up the national mood in a word, I think I would choose the word "frustration".'

We have been finding the going heavy – *very* heavy – for some time. And very uphill too. But what else can we expect when, as a nation, we have deliberately set ourselves to go directly against Almighty God? Deuteronomy 28:20 says that the Lord will do this; the Lord will bring it about. 'The Lord shall send upon thee cursing, vexation [frustration] and rebuke *in all that thou settest thine hand unto, for to do.*' And the reason? 'Because thou hast forsaken Me.'

And it has happened.

8) *And thou shalt become an astonishment, a proverb, and a byword, among all nations.* (v 37) That has happened, hasn't it?

I need not comment further, surely, except perhaps to say that people overseas speak with astonishment that Britain – *Great* Britain – should have been reduced to her present state in such a short period of time. 'It has all happened in about ten years', they say. The result is that we have become a laughing-stock in the eyes of other, less friendly, countries. 'An astonishment, a proverb, and a byword, among all nations.'

And it has happened.

But then, what about this?

9) *The stranger that is within thee shall get up above thee very high; and thou shalt come down very low. He shall lend to thee, and thou shalt not lend to him: he shall be the head, and thou shalt be the tail.* (vv 43,44)

Is not all *that* happening? I would like to quote here from *A Warning to the Nation*: 'Now I want to be very guarded here. The sojourner (or the stranger) that is within thee (or amongst you) is the person of another nationality, of course. In other words, the immigrant.'

And let me say straight away that I will not hear them referred to as foreigners. 'Our friends from overseas', please. I love them. I enjoy being with them. I like their company. I enjoy spending time with them. I am not a racist in any way. But you notice what this verse says: 'He, the immigrant [or stranger that is within thee], shall get above thee very high; and thou shalt come down very low.'

I wrote in *A Warning to the Nation,* 'I am not saying that this has happened in Britain yet, but it *could* happen. And if it does happen, it needs to be recognised as a judgment from God upon the nation. And according to this statement of Scripture, the process could continue until the "stranger that is within thee", the sojourner, the immigrant, has the upper hand in the nation. "He shall be the head, and you shall be the tail".'

Not a few people have written to me recently, saying we are nearer to that now than we were in 1969. And when the situation reaches the *ultimate* stage, men will say, 'It is the finger of God'. You reach the humiliating position where you are obliged, as the host nation, to borrow from the very people that you should be in a position to assist by lending to them. And it is all part of the judgment of God. 'And', I said, 'we have already received warnings that this could be the position in Britain before very long.'

But it is the position in Britain right now, isn't it? 'He shall lend to thee', for instance, 'and thou shalt not lend to him.' By how much is Britain in debt to the Arabs at the present time? By *billions*, not millions? There is no question about it, we are in debt to them up to the hilt. And more and more of our hotels, country and town houses, business premises, shops and stores, and even factories, are being bought up by them.

An indication of how deeply involved we have now become with the Arabs was given in the summer of 1976 when, after that courageous and daring exploit of the Israelis in rescuing the hostages from Entebbe Airport had been successfully carried out, the government of this country maintained a cool silence about it. When country after country was sending its congratulations to the Israeli Government for this marvellous achievement, the British Government, despite all the pressure which was brought to bear, would not express its admiration in any way. And why? For fear that it would offend the Arab world! I see in this a very ominous sign of something terrible that could happen in the future. For should we ever swing so far pro-Arab that we became completely anti-Israel, we could find ourselves involved in a most terrible judgment of God. For Bible students will know that when the final conflagration against Israel – spoken of in detail in Ezekiel 38 and 39, and in the Book of the Revelation chapter 16 – takes place, those nations which range themselves against Israel will be utterly destroyed by a mighty intervention of God on Israel's behalf. And it will take seven years to collect and burn all the devastated weapons, and seven months to collect and bury the dead (Ezekiel 39:9,14).

That verse 44 in Deuteronomy 28 said: 'He shall lend to thee, and thou shalt not lend to him: he shall be the head, and thou shalt be the tail.' In terms of the Arab world, *he* could become so much the head, and could get up so very high above you, Britain – because of your deep financial involvement with him – that you would be obliged to do just what he dictates. And that could mean involvement with him in the very kind of conflagration which the Scriptures describe. But on the wrong side! Is there not an urgent need, therefore, to 'sound the trumpet'?

Each time I read this twenty-eighth chapter of Deuteronomy, it seems to me that more of it applies to our declining national situation. In these verses, we are told that one of the many punishments which will come upon those who will not listen to God, or obey his voice, is that a stranger, or sojourner in our land, will get above us and will hold monetary power over us.

10) But now there comes a *real* crunch. *The fruit of thy land, and all thy labours, shall a nation which thou*

knowest not eat up; and thou shalt be only oppressed and crushed alway. (v 33)

Is not that exactly what has been happening? For what goes on? First, a butter mountain was created. Then a grain mountain. Then a beef mountain. And even a sugar mountain.

And what has been happening to these things in a number of instances? They have been sold at ridiculously cheap prices to the Soviet Union. That is certainly what happened to the butter mountain a few years ago, and there was a mighty furore! It is also what happened to a massive stock-pile of American grain, if not our own. There was a storm in America about that, and it led to an American dock strike, with dockers refusing to load grain on to ships. It is most certainly what happened to our sugar, here in Britain, just before we experienced an acute sugar shortage.

At that time, it was reported in the Press that when the Russians saw that their own sugar-beet crop was going to fail, they sent a trade mission to this country (in the August of that year) and bought up our sugar (500,000 tons of it, I was told) at a ridiculous price. And housewives will remember when it was that the sugar shortage hit us! The *real* reason for the shortage was largely hushed up at the time; otherwise there would have been very angry scenes outside the Houses of Parliament and 10 Downing Street!

'A nation which you have not known shall eat up the fruit of your ground and of all your labours.' But before we start blaming the Russians too much, let us get it straight that God says there is a *reason* why this kind of thing happens to a people. The Bible says that the Lord brings it about. And why? 'Because you have forsaken *me*, people of Britain! It is *because* you have not listened to the voice of the Lord your God to keep his commandments.'

11) *All thy trees and fruit of thy land shall the locust* [or ravaging insect] *consume.* (v 42) Here is another crunch,

– this time in the realm of nature.

You don't need me to remind you that Dutch elm disease has caused havoc in our woodlands, in the countryside, in our local and national parks and gardens, and all along our roadsides. The evidence can be seen all around you, everywhere you go. You don't have to hunt around looking for it! Hundreds of thousands of elm trees have had to be felled, all over the country. Four years ago 3.2 million were dying or dead in the south of England alone. Then in January 1974, oak trees and silver birch started being attacked by an unidentified tree-blight similar to Dutch elm disease. Two years later there were ominous reports of yet another disease attacking our proud English oaks – a disease called tree-wilt.

A little later, in early January 1976, hurricane-force gales which swept across the country snapped off many thousands more trees as if they were matchsticks, and completely uprooted countless others.

That same year came the drought, and *The Times* reported on 4 September 1976 that the effects of that drought had killed millions of trees, and so had added to the past, present, and future disastrous ravages of Dutch elm disease, whilst there had also been devasting effects due to widespread forest fires.

In addition to all that, in both 1974 and 1975, the gardens, fields, hedge-rows, fruit trees, and other trees in the countryside had been so smothered with greenfly, that leaves turned black with greenfly deposits. And the greenfly were there in such great abundance the next year, 1976, that farmers acknowledged that many of the crops in the fields would have been devastated and utterly destroyed had it not been for massive swarms of ladybirds which descended on the greenfly, wherever they were, and proceeded to eat them up. And then, in 1979, the pine trees were in danger of being destroyed by caterpillars.

'All thy trees shall the ravaging insects eat.' And it is happening, isn't it? On a vast scale. Cannot *anybody* read the signs?

Deuteronomy 28:45 says: *All these curses shall come upon thee, and shall pursue thee, and overtake thee, till thou be destroyed: because thou harkenedst not unto the voice of the Lord thy God to keep his commandments and his statutes which He commanded thee.* Then the next verse says: *And they shall be upon thee for a sign.*

For a sign that you are *going the wrong way*. For a sign that you are going directly *against God*. For a sign that the anger of Almighty God has been aroused against you on account of that fact.

When all the uproar was being created in 1976 over the possibility of a film being made in this country about the sex life of Jesus Christ, I noticed that a certain P. F. Brownsey of the Department of Moral Philosophy, University of Glasgow, said in a letter to *The Times*, 'If it could be shown that, in consequence of Mr Thorsen making the film here in Britain, the country will be visited with plagues and famines, then that would be a compelling reason indeed for stopping him, but there is no reason to think such consequences will ensue.'

How blind can a man be? The country is *already* being visited with such things, and has been for some time. The *signs* abound to show us that this is indeed the case. And it would seem that because, like Mr Brownsey, we as a nation have allowed all these signs to go unheeded, then God Almighty sent the further sign, that very year, in the shape of the summer's prolonged drought.

For does he not say in Deuteronomy 11:16, 17: 'Take heed to yourselves, that your heart be not deceived, and ye turn aside, and serve other gods, and worship them; and then the Lord's wrath be kindled against you, and he shut up the heaven, that there be no rain, and that the land yield not her fruit'? And did that not happen in 1976?

What clearer sign could a nation have? When the news went round the world that summer, that the prime minister was calling an emergency cabinet meeting to consider long-term measures to prevent a recurrence of the water shortage which was threatening disaster to all our crops and vital industries, General Amin of Uganda said: 'The present drought is a judgment of God upon Britain'! They called him the Mad Moslem! I found myself saying at the time: 'Yes, God has to use a modern form of Balaam's ass to tell us! We have refused to listen to everybody else. Can't we see?'

Cannot any, or all of our national leaders see? Cannot our gracious Sovereign see?

Cannot those in authority understand, that to reverse a nation's laws and to change its moral and spiritual direction as we have done, so that the country becomes diametrically opposed to what God Almighty has laid down and commanded, is bound to put the nation on a course which is directly against God? But that is precisely what this nation *has* done, and *is* doing.

Is it any wonder that we, as a nation, are not making any headway, or that we seem to be banging our heads against a brick wall? Is it any wonder that we have been bringing down God's judgments upon us, and have had all these things happening to us?

I tell you: Britain and the British people are not likely to make any headway whatsoever, so long as they are going directly *against* Almighty God. The thing is impossible. Not so long as we continue hell-bent on this collision course. Unless we, as a people and as individuals, turn around pretty quickly and seek forgiveness from, and reconciliation with God Almighty, at the foot of the cross of our Lord Jesus Christ, and unless we do it one by one, in true and heartfelt repentance, a terrible crash is inevitable. It will be a crash with the God and Creator of the universe, in terms of some terrible form of judgment never before experienced in the whole of our history. That is the real crisis which is looming up just ahead of us. Let us have no doubt at all about it.

I say, therefore, with all the force that I can muster: There is no other way ahead for our nation, and more particularly for us as individuals, but to turn about – to repent of our sins, to humble ourselves and get ourselves right with Almighty God by asking him for cleansing in the precious blood of the Lord Jesus, one by one, and then to get back to the old paths and tried ways; back to the faith of our fathers. For in *that* way, and only in that way, lies salvation.

All else will be of no avail.

Chapter Eleven
A Nation Ripe for Judgment

So far, we have seen that the *basic* problem with Britain is
that we are a nation living without God, that we are
defying him openly, and are deliberately going against
him.

Now the Bible teaches that if a nation or a people
deliberately continues to go in the kind of direction
Britain is going, persistently and wilfully refusing to heed
the various warnings that God has been giving, then there
comes a time when God has to hand them over to various
other forms of judgment. It says he has to give them up.

Which brings me to the third part of the answer as to
what really is wrong with Britain. *We, as a people, have
got so far away from God in our national rebellion against
him,* that everything points to the fact that *he has already
begun to hand us over* in this kind of way.

The Bible tells us that there are at least five ways in
which God can hand over such a people. I included some
of them in *Pending Judgment on Britain?*[1] Let me now list
all five. He can hand them over to:

1) The gross forms of immorality which are mentioned
in Romans chapter 1.

2) Satan for most severe discipline or, as the New
Testament puts it, 'unto Satan for the destruction of the
flesh' (see 1 Corinthians 5:5; 1 Timothy 1:20).

3) Some great national catastrophe. (Daniel 9:12-14)
4) Enemies within. (Judges 2:13-15)
5) An enemy who is threatening from without. (Deuteronomy 28:47-52)

1) In Romans 1, for instance, we find that because they refused to acknowledge God (*refused* to, notice), '*God also gave them up to uncleanness . . . to dishonour their own bodies between themselves . . . God gave them up unto vile affections: for even their women did change the natural use into that which is against nature; and likewise also the men, leaving the natural use of the woman, burned in their lust one toward another . . . receiving in themselves that recompence of their error which was meet. And even as they did not like to retain God in their knowledge, God gave them over to a reprobate mind, to do those things which are not convenient; being filled with all unrighteousness . . . Who, knowing the judgment of God, that they which commit such things are worthy of death, not only do the same, but have pleasure in them that do them.* (Romans 1:24-32)

Three times over in this passage we read that 'God gave them up': 'God gave them up to uncleanness' (v 24). 'God gave them up unto vile affections' (v 26). 'God gave them over to a reprobate mind' (v 28).

All this is referred to in verse 18 as 'the wrath of God' being 'revealed from heaven against all ungodliness and unrighteousness of men'; which means that 'the handing over' to all these obnoxious and distasteful things that are mentioned in this chapter, is a very definite form of God's judgment. We need to remember that, people of Britain, when we see all these things proliferating around us.

The chapter goes on to say that such people 'receive in their own persons the due penalty for their error.' (v 27, RSV) You do not need me to tell you of the gross immorality with which our country is riddled today. British medical records and reports all show that venereal disease in Britain, even amongst the young, has reached the proportions of a national epidemic: 'receiving in their own persons that recompence of their error which was meet.'

Has God had to hand us over, as a nation, to this, because we refuse to find any place for him in our national life, or because we do not see fit to acknowledge him, and refuse to have anything to do with him *as individuals?* One of the most knowledgeable and highly qualified doctors in this country informed some of us, at a recent meeting of concerned people, that instructions are now being given to hospital staffs, stressing the need to take throat swabs from certain patients to check the possible existence of a particularly abhorrent form of venereal disease in that part of the body. This deeply disturbing report carries its own ghastly implications.

This is the extent to which people are receiving in their own persons the due rewards of their deeds. They are literally destroying themselves as a result of their extremely loose behaviour.

Doesn't *somebody* need to 'sound the trumpet'?

2) The New Testament talks in more than one place of *God having to hand certain individuals over to Satan for severe discipline,* even for the destruction of the flesh, if they still refuse to repent. And this is because of their extreme wilfulness (1 Corinthians 5:5; 1 Timothy 1:20).

When I first read this in the Bible I could not bring myself ever to mention it in public. But now I must ask: Does God sometimes have to hand *nations* over to this kind of thing? That question becomes increasingly important in view of the ever-tightening grip which Satanism, spiritism, witchcraft, the black arts, and all other forms of the occult are getting on this country.

The question is relevant, too, in view of the way the people of this country are being constantly bombarded with films about demon-possessed people and exorcism;

about the activities of all the evil powers of darkness, not only in our cinemas but on television; and because of the way these evil practices are discussed on the radio, and even in our schools.

I can never forget how a few years ago, when I was speaking in Oxford along these lines, the rural dean asked me if I would be prepared to talk to a meeting of the clergy in the city. When I asked him why he was so anxious to arrange this, he said it was because he was deeply concerned about the number of people in Oxford who were being initiated into various forms of Satanism and demon-worship every week. He used the word 'initiated', which means going the whole way – committing themselves fully. This, in blunt English, means 'selling themselves, or handing themselves completely over' to the devil. He quoted a figure which, by any count, was extremely alarming. In fact, working out the figure on the way home, the numbers involved were such that I found myself saying, 'If that number of people in Oxford were being converted to faith in Jesus Christ every week, there would be headline news in the national Press telling us that a revival of Christianity had hit one of our major university cities.'

Then this possibility dawned on me: He did not say these people who were being initiated were from the university. He said they were people 'in Oxford'. But they could have included people from the university, and no doubt did. As that alarming figure continued to take hold of my mind I thought: could it possibly be that initiation continues at this rate, we shall find that in ten or twenty years time the occupant of 10 Downing Street is a demon-possessed person? After all, it is the universities which produce most of our future national leaders: our politicians, our professional men, our teachers, our business magnates – in short, most of the influential people of the future.

It happened in Nazi Germany, friends! Those in

authority during the Nazi regime were demon-possessed. Hitler was a demon-possessed person (Rommel, in his papers, describes him as 'the devil-incarnate'). Goebbels was demon-possessed; so was the leader of the SS, many of the SS men, and other of the Nazi leaders. Their very emblem, the swastika, is a symbol of satanical powers.

We should not delude ourselves into believing that it could not possibly happen in this country. Shortly after my Oxford experience, I was in Yorkshire, and learnt on very good authority that a number of witches' covens had just met under a full moon in a forest in Yorkshire, with nearly a thousand people present – and that they had all arrived in Rolls, Daimlers, Jaguars and such like! And in September 1976 a Fleet Street investigation revealed that there are witches who claim that secret covens exist in every big town in the land!

3) *God could visit us with some great national calamity.* In *Pending Judgment on Britain,* I drew attention to the real possibility of one such catastrophe happening. That was the possibility of London being destroyed by a flood.

The British Press has been giving warnings for a number of years, and Lord Bowden, principal of the University of Manchester Institute of Science and Technology, has drawn urgent attention to it when opening a debate in the House of Lords on 'Flood Prevention in the Thames'. He put it in this way.

London has been sinking by a foot every 100 years. The tides have been rising by eighteen inches ever 100 years. Existing flood barriers are sinking under their own weight into the London clay. The barrier confronting the Thames in front of the Houses of Parliament, said Lord Bowden, was two feet lower than 100 years ago. Every so many years there is a tidal surge in the Atlantic which, when the wind is in a certain direction (mainly NW), gets driven round the northern coast of Scotland down into the North

Sea. A big build-up of water occurs. This is accentuated by the Channel, which forms a 'bottle-neck' and prevents the water escaping fast enough into the Atlantic again. The Thames estuary forms a natural gateway through which the excess water rushes. But if this surge coincides with high tides, a full moon, and with the wind in a north-westerly direction – because the wind prevents one high tide in the Thames from ebbing before the next tide is due in – an inevitable high rise in the level of water results all the way up to London, and, having no other means of escape, it must either burst existing banks and river walls, or over-top them. Such a possibility is very real.

Should such a surge occur, an area from Wapping to Richmond, and from the Thames Embankment right across to Kings Cross could be flooded, and in some places to a depth of ten feet or more. This would mean that much of London's Underground system would be put out of action; telecommunication and electrical systems would be seriously affected; damage to property could amount to £1,000 million pounds worth, with a further £1,000 million pounds worth of derivative damage; and there could be very considerable loss of life. London, as a capital city, could be put out of effective action for as long as six to nine months.

At the end of his address Lord Bowden quoted this very significant sentence: 'The angel of death is abroad in the land, and we may almost hear the beating of his wings.' This is the language of judgment.

Lest anyone should be tempted to believe that this danger has now receded, constant warnings have since been issued that the danger is increasing, not diminishing. It could still happen within the next few years, until the flood barrier at Woolwich is completed. London is, in fact, living on borrowed time.[2]

You may ask why I say that, if such a catastrophic event were to happen, it should be seen as a judgment of God upon Britain? In what sense would this be true?

Because of what I find in Daniel chapter 9: *All this calamity* (evil, AV) *has come upon us, yet we have not prayed unto the Lord our God, turning from our iniquities and giving heed to thy truth. Therefore the Lord has kept ready the calamity and has brought it upon us* (Daniel 9:13-14, RSV).

When Daniel said 'all this calamity', he meant all the *previous* calamity which had come upon his people and upon his nation in recent years. 'All this previous calamity has come upon us', is what he is really saying, 'and yet we have not prayed unto the Lord our God . . . Therefore the Lord has kept ready the calamity [this present one] and has brought it upon us.' That is the full force of his words. So what is their relevance to Britain's situation today?

Daniel lived at a time when the nation was undergoing the judgments of God because it had turned away from him, was rebelling against him, and had ignored his commandments. Because it was a nation under judgment, Daniel had seen it suffer one calamity after another. Its people had sinned and done wickedly (v 5): *that* was the reason.

Yet it still continued along the path of defiance without giving any regard to God whatsoever. Daniel put the full case before the Lord in his prayer; here it is. Notice, as you read it, how much of what he said is relevant to our own situation today.

We have sinned, and have committed iniquity, and have done wickedly, and have rebelled, even by turning aside from thy commandments and from thy ordinances.

Neither have we hearkened unto thy servants the prophets, which spake in thy name to our rulers . . . and to all the people of the land . . . To us, O Lord, belongs confusion of face, and to our rulers . . . because we have sinned against thee. . . . Because we have rebelled . . . and have not obeyed the voice of the Lord our God by following his laws which he set before us.

All Israel [the whole nation, that is] *has transgressed thy law, and turned aside, refusing to obey thy voice.*

And the curse and the oath which are written in the law of Moses the servant of God [Deuteronomy 28 in particular] *have been poured out upon us, because we have sinned against him. He has confirmed his words, which he spoke against us and against our rulers by bringing upon us a great calamity* (Daniel 9:5-12, RSV).

Having put this case before the Lord, Daniel says: 'All this evil is come upon us: yet [*and yet*] made we not our prayer before the Lord our God . ... Therefore the Lord has brought this further calamity upon us which he has been keeping ready' (vv 13, 14). Which is precisely Britain's case. We have suffered God's judgments one after another (each one of those contained in Deuteronomy 28; those which comprise the curse and the oath in the law of Moses the servant of God. We have suffered one national calamity after another, and yet . . . and yet . . . we have persistently and stubbornly refused to pray to the Lord our God as a nation – as a people.

Times without number, urgent appeals have been sent by organisations and individuals, including myself, to the Sovereign, to call the nation to God in prayer as His Majesty King George VI did between 1939 and 1945. Every time the result has been the same. Each successive prime minister (who advises the Sovereign) has replied: 'The situation does not demand it.'

Even the last Archbishop of Canterbury (Dr Donald Coggan), having admitted in print that ever since he took office he had had a steady stream of letters coming in and calling for a Day of Prayer for the Nation (and one of his executives has written that 'One has to record a certain wonder at the sheer volume of pressure for such a Day in the Archbishop's letters') – even the last Archbishop, despite all this weight of demand from so many people, has said, in conjunction with the Archbishop of York: 'A "Call to Prayer" would not be the same as thirty years ago, because the tone of British society since World War II has become less and less traditionally Christian.' Therefore, 'such a call is not likely to be heeded by more than 10 per cent of the nation.' And so that great volume of requests has been rejected on these pathetic grounds. Presumably the advice which has been given to the Sovereign is the same.

I notice that there is no reference whatsoever to the possibility of such a Call to Prayer being heeded *by Almighty God*!

A further appeal was made, by many people, for the nation to be called to God in prayer when the effect of the prolonged drought experienced in Britain throughout the summer of 1976 became extremely acute. Once again the appeal was rejected. The great name of God Almighty, the real controller of the weather, was brought still further into disrepute when it was left to the Sikhs who are living amongst us, out of their deep concern about the drought, to send to the Punjab for their holy men to come and hold a three-day rain-making festival in London in an effort to break it. And God's name was still further mocked when the BBC gleefully announced that the Sikhs were cock-a-hoop because, after but one day of their rain-making festival, London had its first rain in months, and various parts of the country had floods and deluges. 'They had done what nobody else had been able to do.'

Is not this what God himself refers to in the Old Testament as profaning his holy name among the heathen (Ezekiel 36:22)? I would think it is, especially when, only twenty-four hours afterwards, a leading national newspaper carried the headline: 'Archbishop of Canterbury Rejects Call to Prayer'. The stubbornness of the nation's Christian leaders was continuing.

It still continued, even when the Chief Rabbi published a letter in *The Times* saying that the Jewish community had been praying to God in their synagogues for rain.

'All this evil is come upon us', said Daniel, 'yet cried we not unto the Lord our God.' Are we not in exactly the same position as that outlined in Daniel's prayer in chapter 9? Surely there is good reason for saying that were such a catastrophic event to take place as the destruction of our capital by the Thames bursting its banks, it should be seen as a judgment of God upon Britain? 'All these *previous* calamities have come upon us [all those already referred to, including the drought], and yet cried we not unto the Lord our God.' God might well be *keeping ready* such a calamity as this, and could bring it upon us if we *still* refuse to turn from our iniquities and turn to him in humble repentance and prayer.

We are in a 'Daniel chapter 9' situation. But the national calamity need not necessarily take the form of a flood disaster in the Thames. It could take some other form.

a) *The total collapse of our national economy.* For a number of years now our political leaders have been warning us of such a possibility. This is the crash which *they* forsee.

b) *The failure of our entire industrial system.* Sir Maurice Laing has already warned us of the possibility of *that* happening, when he said, 'What we are about to witness is the total collapse of our entire industrial system.'

c) *The total disintegration of the United Kingdom.* The ingredients of that kind of judgment are already there. This theme will be expanded further in Volume 3.

d) *The total loss of our North Sea oil,* on which our leaders have so confidently come to depend, but which is by no means secure – especially when the Soviet Union runs short of oil early in the 1980s!

e) *The total collapse of the whole cultural structure of our society* as we know it. Indeed I see Britain today like a building from which all the cement and mortar are fast being removed. The cement and mortar are the essential Christian foundations and standards which, until recent years, have bonded Britain's structure. Remove the cement and mortar from between the bricks of *any* building and the total collapse of that building is inevitable. Even so with a nation.

Indeed, a recent writer has warned that the whole of western culture is now collapsing. 'Such a collapse', he says, 'is something that we in Britain have never experienced in its totality for centuries, *but we are beginning to see signs of such a critical event.*'[3]

4) The Bible teaches that *God can also hand a people over to enemies within*. The Book of Judges tells us that 'when Israel did evil yet again in the sight of the Lord, he delivered them into the hands of spoilers that spoiled them, and he sold them into the hands of their enemies round about' (Judges 2:14). In the context in which it happened, this meant the enemies within their borders. He delivered them into the hands of enemies who were at work *within the realm* – enemies who were out to disrupt, overthrow, destroy, take over.

We read that Israel was utterly powerless to make any kind of stand against them. Britain is suffering at the hands of such people today. It has happened continuously within British Leyland. But many voices have been raised in warning over a long period of time, including those on the shop-floors of our factories, as well as those of our national leaders.

The 'enemy within' has entered practically every branch of our national life, including MI5 and MI6.[4] Our industry and trade unions have been well and truly infiltrated; so have our universities, schools, and teacher-training colleges. Local and national government, the BBC and the Civil Service have all been penetrated. And since world statesmen, including foreign ministers, say that there has been a very high degree of communist infiltration into most of the world's churches, it is more than likely that our own churches have been affected.

Then there is always a very real possibility of a confrontation between the trade unions and the Government, leading to a take-over of this country by powerful and extreme elements of the Left Wing, who are bent on bringing in communist policies under what would then be their own communist government. That danger has been confronting the country for years, is being orchestrated from Moscow, and could be what all this infiltration is about.

Let us never forget that to bring about the total collapse of a nation's economy, the failure of its entire industrial system, and the total disintegration of a nation itself, is all part of the work of the 'enemies within' in order to bring about their intended aim. As former President Nixon has written in his recently published book *The Real War*, 'Local communist parties and communist-headed unions, by leading strikes, by demanding excessive wage increases, by calling for nationalisation of industries and by sponsoring terrorism amongst businessmen, can damage the investment climate of a country so badly that money will stop flowing in. Their Soviet masters thrive on chaos, confusion and fear. They know that economic depression, revolution and war can destroy the fabric of any society. Therefore they try, by whatever means they can, to exacerbate tensions throughout the world, stir up discontent, foment wars and revolution. The Russians do not want human needs met. They do not want problems solved. They want problems to escalate *in order to seize the nation.*'[5] (my italics)

Britain today is most certainly faced with a very real danger from such enemies – powerful enemies – at work within its borders, some of them just waiting for the right moment to effect a take-over, with or without the assistance of the Soviet Union. We are a prime target for such an attempt.

So I ask: Is this a judgment of God, because, as a nation, we are flying in his face, and openly defying him, after all the good that he has lavished upon us through the centuries of our history?

Judgment could take any or all of these forms. It could even take a form more severe than any of them, or of all of them put together.

5) *For Britain today is also confronted with the very real danger of an enemy from without.* Mrs Margaret Thatcher is by no means the only one who has been raising a voice about the build-up of overwhelming forces in the Soviet Union and Warsaw Pact countries, against which NATO forces form, or should form, the major part of the Western Europe's, and so of Britain's defensive shield. For years now the voices of NATO's most senior officers have been heard, both in and outside Britain, warning all concerned of Russia's intentions and ever-increasing strength: not least those of General Goodpaster, Supreme Commander, NATO forces in Europe; General Alexander Haig; Dr Joseph Luns, Secretary-General of NATO and chairman of the North Atlantic Council; and our own General Sir Walter Walker and Air Chief Marshal Sir Neil Cameron.

More recently, further stringent warnings have been sounded out. Dr Kissinger, for instance, wrote in his recently published memoirs: 'The world stands once again on the brink of military confrontation.' Then he said in Brussels in September 1979: 'The time of greatest peril for Western Europe will be 1982-86, when the Soviet Union's massive defence spending will bear fruit and permit Moscow to jump ahead in military capability.' His sombre words continued: 'The Soviet Union is rapidly achieving superiority over the West in every category of military strength. On present trends, this superiority will be at its most decisive *early in the 1980s.*' (my italics) He then gave this warning: 'In the entire history of the world, no nation has ever achieved such superiority without seeking to translate it into foreign political advantage.'

On 6 October 1979, General Walker sounded the alarm

once more. Speaking in London on 'The Defence of the West against the Soviet Global Threat' – which he illustrated profusely by military wall-charts – he said: 'Never has the world situation been so grave and dangerous since World War II. The Soviet Union's mood is now one of war, as they drive forward to accomplish their objective – which is world domination. We are thus moving into a high-risk period which will be all the more dangerous because of Soviet realisation that their military superiority may be fairly short lived. The temptation to press on will be very great. NATO is now so outnumbered, outgunned and outstripped in every direction that the Soviet Union may well be tempted to flex her muscles.' 'Dr Kissinger', declared General Walker, 'has suggested 1982 as the likely date for this to happen, less than three years off. Other analysts have argued that it may be even sooner than that.'

Then he said: 'The stark reality is that Great Britain and Western Europe over the next three to four years are going to be in supreme danger. We could be facing surrender or defeat by 1982!'

This is to be in a 'Book of Jeremiah' situation. Bible students will know what I mean. General Walker stressed that 'The hour is very late. It may well be too late to prevent the Soviets from striking at England, which could come simultaneously with an attack in the Middle East.'

That was the warning being sounded out last October. But when the news broke at Christmas-time last year that Russian forces had invaded Afghanistan, the alarm bells began to ring all over Europe. They began to ring all over the Middle East as well, because of the Russian threat to Middle East oil wells.

A further clear warning was sounded out as recently as the weekend of 15-16 March 1980. At this time the warning was issued by a very senior *Soviet* general who has sought asylum in the United States. This Russian officer, General Grigorenko, had already been claiming a year ago that Europe would be Russia's next target once the Kremlin had achieved, with Cuban help, its aims in Africa. Now, in the spring of 1980, he issued a warning that the Soviet Union may take military action against Europe before the end of *this* year. He claimed that the Soviet invasion of Afghanistan at the beginning of the year had been a test of the West's capacity for reaction: 'The operation was successful. The western camp is divided.' Then the general said: 'Afghanistan may prove in coming weeks to have been the "detonation" of war with incalculable consequences – a Third World War in fact.' He added, 'I think this will probably happen before the end of the year. Then we will be able to test the theory that Russian troops can cross Germany in three hours.'

These are only some of the warnings given. So who can deny that Britain today is confronted with the very real danger of an enemy from without?

Furthermore, the threat does not only come from overland to the Channel ports and beyond; or from aerial bombardment; or from the 130 or more SS20 medium-range nuclear missiles which the Soviets now have deployed on their extreme western border, each having a range of 2,200 miles and carrying three independently targeted nuclear warheads capable of hitting any target in Western Europe from Gibraltar to the North Cape right up in north Norway – which brings London well within range – and against which there is no western response.

There is the very real threat to all our sea-lines of communication. They could easily be closed by powerful units of the Soviet Navy which are already sitting astride them. For instance, as a result of phenomenal naval expansion and of pushing the naval defence line out beyond Iceland, Russia now has naval forces in position which are capable of closing the sea-passages between the north coast of Scotland and Iceland, including the vital Denmark straits, and of shutting off such sea-routes to and from Britain as the Atlantic approaches, the western approaches, and the Irish Sea. Since Russian electronic intelligence trawlers and submarines operate an almost continuous patrol around the coasts of Britain, and since the Russian backfire bombers are capable of attacking shipping in the Atlantic as far south as the Azores from their bases in Northern Russia, and of returning home without refuelling, there is a very real threat of Britain being blockaded at sea. There is also the possibility of an additional blockade: the threat to the sea-routes leading from the Persian Gulf and round the Cape of South Africa. Were these sea passages to be closed, it would mean that our food and oil supplies would be cut off and all our industry and fighting forces would grind to a standstill, leaving this country with no alternative but to surrender to domination by a foreign power.

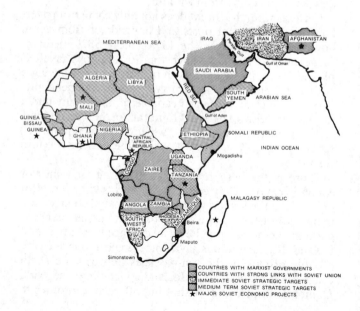

This is the form of national calamity which I fear most of all; and this is why I believe the trumpet should be sounded loud and clear. Were these blockades to happen, it should be seen as very much a judgment of God upon the nation for all our wickedness in forsaking him.

As to exactly what Russia's long and short-term aims with regard to the Cape route are, one of the men in a position to know, probably better than most, is General Sir Walter Walker. He has held two appointments, first as Deputy Chief-of-Staff in charge of plans, operations and intelligence, Allied Forces Central Europe, and then as Commander-in-Chief of Allied Forces Northern Europe. Writing in his bi-monthly paper, *International Summary*, he said: 'I want to state quite categorically and with due solemnity, that Russia intends, by blackmail, revolutionary war by proxy, or by brute force, to absorb the whole of South Africa, deprive the West of vital minerals, and control Europe's life-line round the Cape . . . What is now at stake is not only the whole future of Western Europe, but civilisation itself and the western way of life.'

No less emphatic were the comments of Mr Van Der Byl, a former minister of defence and foreign affairs in what is now Zimbabwe: 'I am firmly convinced, as I believe most thinking people in the world are convinced, that the Soviet tactic is to get hold of the Cape sea-route, and in the process, as much of Africa as possible . . . If they were to take the whole of Southern Africa, which is clearly their intention in one way or another, then of course the position of Western Europe and the NATO countries and the rest would be pretty perilous. Now this is what I believe the whole thing is about. All the indications are there, and nobody denies it.'

Much more recently, no less a person than the Soviet President, Leonid Brezhnev, confirmed this when he said to Somalian President Siad Barre, who was then an ally of the USSR: 'Our aim is to gain control of the two great treasure houses on which the West depends – the energy treasure house of the Persian Gulf, and the mineral treasure house of central and southern Africa.'[6]

So now we know. There is nothing like having it straight from the horse's mouth, or the mouth of the Red Bear for that matter!

As for the threat to the Persian Gulf area and the Middle East oil wells, Richard Nixon says: 'In the near future the Soviet Union may need Persian Gulf oil as their domestic supplies dwindle.

'Never has the region of the Persian Gulf been so vital to the future of the world; never have the nations of the Persian Gulf been so vulnerable to an aggressive power that seeks to impose its will on the world. If the Soviets succeed in taking effective control of the Persian Gulf, Europe and Japan will be at their mercy – and mercy is not one of their most notable virtues.'[7] Furthermore he says, 'The Soviet Union's ultimate target is its chief rival, the United States. Its *intermediate* targets are Western Europe and Japan.'[8]

So the danger to this country of the 'enemy without' is very real, for there is no need to remind the reader that Western Europe includes Britain.

In Daniel's day, the great calamity which the Lord first kept ready, and then brought upon the nation because its people and its leaders persistently refused to return to him, took the form of the overthrow of the capital by a foreign power, followed by total domination. In view of the way *our* nation has departed today, why should *we* expect anything less?

It was a Royal Naval commander who said to me some years ago: 'Something *serious* has got to happen to bring this country to its knees. *Preaching* won't do it any more. Neither will evangelism.' Then, almost in a whisper, he said, 'God may have to use Russia!'

I myself have been warning over the years of the *spiritual* implications of the colossal build-up of Soviet forces and of their threat to Britain and the West, by giving addresses – some of two or three hour's duration – in many different places. And I have backed them up with literature (which has been, and is being, widely distributed) and with tape-recorded messages.

It is about the *spiritual* implications of this build-up that we, as a people, need most to be warned. Deuteronomy 28:47-8 – that same chapter in which all those other curses and judgments are listed – goes on to say: '*Because* thou servedst not the Lord thy God with joyfulness, and with gladness of heart, for the abundance of all things; *therefore* shalt thou serve thine enemies which the Lord shall send against thee.'

'*Because* you do not serve the Lord your God . . . you shall serve your enemies.'

Then we read that 'The *Lord* shall bring a nation against thee from afar, from the end of the earth, as swift as the eagle flieth; a nation whose tongue thou shalt not understand; a nation of a fierce countenance' (Deuteronomy 28:49-50).

'The *Lord* shall', is what it says. For it should be clearly understood that the Bible makes it very plain that God sometimes uses *nations* as his instruments of judgment. For instance, in the early books of the Bible he used the nation of Israel as his instrument of judgment against the notorious Amorites, when the iniquity of the Amorites had come to the full. Then in the later books of the Old Testament, when the iniquity of the nation of Israel itself had reached a very high peak, God raised up nations as his instruments of judgment against *her*. There was Assyria, for instance, and then Nebuchadnezzar and the armies of Babylon.

I believe God does this in a modern age, too. I am prepared to say that God used Britain as an instrument of judgment against Nazi Germany when, under Hitler's influence and leadership, the Third Reich became so indescribably evil, tyrannical and wicked. He certainly used Britain and the combined forces of the Allies as his instrument of *deliverance* when the appointed time had come to deliver the people of the Continent from the hands of a raging maniac.

So we should not be at all surprised if, because of Britain's present departure from God and wilful defiance of him, he is raising up a powerful nation as an instrument of judgment against *her*.

It has happened before in history. In the Book of Judges chapter 3:12 we read: 'And the children of Israel did evil again in the sight of the Lord . . . the Lord strengthened . . . the King of Moab against Israel, because they had done evil in the sight of the Lord.' They had to serve the King of Moab for eighteen years, and that, indeed, could even be the *spiritual* implication behind the colossal Soviet build-up. If so, the verse could read, 'The Lord strengthened the Soviet Union against Britain because they had done evil in the sight of the Lord.'

Notice that the *Lord* did this. 'The *Lord* strengthened . . . ' So my case, in answer to the question 'What *really* is wrong with Britain?', is this:

1) We are a nation living without God, and without any reference to God.
2) We are openly defying him and wilfully flying in his face.
3) We have got so far away from God, as a nation, that we have already become a nation under judgment, and in terms of such judgment have begun to be 'handed over' and to be 'given up' in a number of ways.
4) All the indications are that unless we turn to God and repent, there is a further and more grievous judgment being kept ready for us, and which will be brought upon us. And that judgment could take the form of our being handed over to a foreign power, or of being brought to such a position as to leave us with no alternative but to surrender and to submit to

foreign domination.

My case, furthermore, is that it is no longer a question as to *whether* we have departed from God. That we *have* done so is beyond dispute, and it is now a question of *how far* we have departed. In Volumes 2 and 3 I shall seek to show that.

we have departed from God *historically,*
we have departed from God *spiritually* and *morally,*
we have departed from God *politically* and *legally,* and
we have departed from God *constitutionally.*

NOTES

1. An address delivered by the author at NATO HQ in Rheindahlen, Germany, at the request of its commanding officer, and which has since been available in leaflet form, going into over 100,000 copies.
2. For a graphic account of what *could* happen, read Richard Doyle's novel *Deluge,* Arlington Books, 3 Clifford Street, Mayfair, London W1, 1976.
3. O.R. Johnston, *Christianity in a Collapsing Culture,* Paternoster Press, 3 Mount Radford Crescent, Exeter, 1976.
4. See, for instance, Chapman Pincher's book, *Inside Story,* Sidgwick and Jackson, 1 Tavistock Chambers, Bloomsbury Way, London WC1, 1978, chapters 1, 8 and 9 in particular.
5. Richard Nixon, *The Real War,* Sidgwick and Jackson, London, 1980. Quoted from serialised version published in *Now* magazine, 11-17 April 1980 edition, p23.
6. *Now* magazine, 11-17 April 1980 edition, p19.
7. ibid., p21.
8. ibid., pp18-19.

Acknowledgements

I list with grateful acknowledgements the various publications which I have consulted during the preparation of this book, and from which some of the material has been drawn.

Books

Winston S. Churchill, *History of the English-speaking Peoples,* Volume 1, Cassell, London 1956.

G. M. Trevelyan, *A Shortened History of England,* Pelican, London 1970.

J. Wesley Bready, *England Before and After Wesley,* Hodder and Stoughton, London 1939.

George Whitefield's Journals, The Banner of Truth Trust, Edinburgh 1960.

Richard Doyle, *Deluge* (novel), Arlington Books, London 1976.

O. R. Johnston, *Christianity in a Collapsing Culture,* Paternoster Press, Exeter 1976.

Chapman Pincher, *Inside Story,* Sidgwick and Jackson, London 1978.

Richard Nixon, *The Real War,* Sidgwick and Jackson, London 1980.

The Rommel Papers, ed. B. H. Liddell Hart, Collins, London 1953.

John Poulton, *Dear Archbishop,* Hodder and Stoughton, London 1976.

Leaflets, Magazines and Pamphlets

General Sir Walter Walker, *International Summary.*

Now magazine, 11-17 April 1980.

The Rev. David E. Gardner, *Pending Judgment on Britain,* an address delivered at the NATO Headquarters, Rheindahlen, Germany.

The Rev. David E. Gardner, *A Warning to the Nation,* Christian Foundation Publications, eighth reprint. Available from 45 Appleton Road, Hale, Altrincham, Cheshire.

I would also like to place on record grateful thanks and deep appreciation to all those who have helped with the typing and re-typing of this manuscript and those of Volumes 2 and 3. They include Miss Eileen Devenish, formerly of Twickenham, Middlesex, who undertook the mammoth task of typing a large part of the original manuscript in triplicate; Mrs Margaret Williamsen of Wantage, Oxon, who gallantly took over at a later stage; and more recently Mrs Margaret Greaves of Wandsworth.

I am also greatly indebted to Miss Gwen Saunders for the very valuable help which she has given over a considerable period of time, and to Lance Bidewell for the painstaking and thorough way in which he has scrutinised the text of Volume 1 and given generous help and advice in preparation for its publication.

Also to Rodney Shepherd of Nuprint Services, whose personal Christian commitment led to an interest in the message, resulting in its attractive presentation as the printed word.

Last, but by no means least, I would like to express my grateful appreciation to Dr Brian Taylor of Altrincham, Cheshire, for recognising the extreme urgency and relevance of the message and deciding to go ahead with the utmost possible speed with its publication. Without his generous and courageous help the book may never have seen the light of day.